TREES AND A CHERRY TREE

This is a reproduction of a bit of colour 'fun' that I had one late afternoon in February.
Why I am talking a little about colour in a book on drawing is explained on pages 14–21.

DRAWING
FOR CHILDREN AND OTHERS

VERNON BLAKE

LONDON : HUMPHREY MILFORD

OXFORD UNIVERSITY PRESS

1927

Oxford University Press
London   Edinburgh   Glasgow   Copenhagen
New York Toronto Melbourne Cape Town
Bombay Calcutta Madras Shanghai
Humphrey Milford Publisher to the UNIVERSITY

TABLE OF CONTENTS

PREFACE. FOR THE 'OTHERS' . . . vii

Idea of the book. The child's imagination. Reasons for advising study of Nature. Drawing is seeing. Observation. Simple language. Difference between a good picture and a bad one. Drawing the basis of painting. A drawing is finished before it is begun. Tidiness. Perseverance. Egypt and China. Beauty and enthusiasm. Drawing is not copying. Beauty the beginning and end of art.

CHAPTER I. WHAT DRAWING IS . . . I

Learning to draw is learning to see. Scribbling can be good drawing. Scribble from Nature because you must learn to see. What to notice. Shadows often more important than things themselves. We must take a keen delight in practising art. Do not rub out. Look at the object and not at your drawing. We cannot know too much about how things are made. Use thin, cheap paper and make hundreds of drawings. Differing *importance* of facts which we observe. What is meant by 'importance'?

CHAPTER II. WHAT TO DRAW . . . 22

What shall we draw? this matters a great deal. Do not copy flat 'copies'. The aim of painting is to represent bodies in relief on a flat surface (Leonardo da Vinci). Ground-plan. Do not draw big 'views'. Draw simple subjects. Difficulty of 'seeing' a good subject. Do not put things in the middle of the paper. Balance. 'The Fisherman' by Claude Lorrain. Its 'composition' or 'pattern' taken to pieces. Draw things which interest you. Make scribbles (not copies) from Great Masters' pictures. Always draw from solid objects. Rhythm or 'coming naturally after'. Music. All parts of a picture must be satisfactorily 'joined up'. A balanced 'scribble' is a good drawing; an unbalanced tidy drawing is not a drawing at all. Only study the works of the greatest masters. Great drawings are not tidy. 'Pattern' is everything, and should go *into* the paper as well as *over* it.

CHAPTER III.   WHAT TO DRAW WITH   .   .   47

It does not matter what you draw with.   Do a great number of drawings ; they will get slowly better.   Do not correct ; do another. Draw freely.   Pencil.   Pen.   Charcoal.   Brush.   Learn the habit of making drawings, not of correcting them.   Water-colour washes. Know what you are going to do before you do it.

CHAPTER IV.   SHAPES OF THINGS .   .   .   54

' Important' shapes and ' unimportant' shapes.   Cézanne.   Geometrical construction.   Perspective.   Drawing a street.   The Horizon Line.   Vanishing Point.   Linear Perspective is one of the ways of making drawings look 'solid'.   Aerial Perspective. Values.   Three ways of making drawings look 'solid'.   Detail must ' lie over ' solidity.   Leaving things out.   'Solidity' of tree foliage.   Bad pictures.   Why trees are chosen as models.

   Explanation of a perspective diagram : Height of Horizon Line. Vanishing Points.   Distance Points.   Drawing on a pane of glass.

CHAPTER V.   CONCERNING A CHESTNUT TREE   .   77

Your drawing shows what you have thought.   Do not copy my diagrams.   Draw from a real tree.   Do not draw ugly things ; art is beauty.   A tree trunk is cylindrical.   Height of the Horizon Line is of first 'importance'.   How to find it.   Never draw anything without being sure just how it comes towards you or goes away from you.   Study a few things properly, not many carelessly.   Draw nothing you have not studied.   ' Musical feeling ' in drawing.   ' Musical ' growth of trees.   Many kinds of beauty. Drawing is a statement of beauty.   Beauty of architecture.   Ictinos and Pheidias.   Parthenon.   Nature.   Geometry and suppleness. Mechanics of form.   Planes.   Faults of bad drawings.   What you feel will come out at the tip of your brush.   ' Lop-sided ' composition.   Need of foreground.   Comparison of values.   Foreground and pattern.

CHAPTER VI.   A DRAWING OF A CHESTNUT TREE   96

Do not copy this drawing.   Musical harmonies and rhythm. Drawing is not imitation ; it is getting excited about rhythms, about patterns.   A photographic apparatus has only one 'eye'. Linear perspective wants in solidity.   Why we 'see solid' with two eyes. How to use 'stereoscopic vision' in drawing. We cannot 'get excited' about a photograph. Leaving out. As much pattern *into* the paper as *on* it. Why the drawing is not more finished. What I used.

CHAPTER VII. THE BEAUTY OF THE PINE   .   109
Symbolic meanings of things in Chinese paintings. The main facts of the 'pattern' of the photograph reproduced. 'Holes' in a pattern. Everything must fit into the pattern. The 'springing' out of the ground of a tree. Draw 'likeness' to movement.

CHAPTER VIII. PATTERN. FINISH. TECHNIQUE .   117
More about what to draw. Leave off drawing a bad pattern. It is easier to do a good drawing than to do a bad one. Only work according to the needs of your pattern. Turner's rapid sketches. The 'first fine careless rapture'. Good advice and bad advice. What attracts our attention to a subject? Technique and subject. Early Italian painters and Rembrandt. The reason of a sketch. Uninteresting things well arranged make a better picture than interesting things badly arranged. A picture is an arrangement. Drawing and picture-making are one and the same thing. 'In-artistic' exercises will never teach you to draw. A bad 'pattern' corrected. Without having a good pattern I do not know how to draw, I do not know what lines to make. Radiation in branches. Important foreground.

CHAPTER IX. CONCLUSION   .   .   .   134
Drawing is a statement of beauty. What is beauty? Do not pay attention to modern painters' work, until you know yourself how to judge of its worth. The 'scribbly' nature of many great artists' drawings. Prophecies. A short history of recent art: The Impressionists. Cézanne. Van Gogh. Henri Matisse. Cubists. The future: Constructive drawing. Beautiful emotion. The error of the Cubists. The underlying technique. The 'stone-yard' of a drawing. Solid construction underlies beauty. Beauty is not flimsy. Finish is refined additional observation. Draw anything which seems to you to make a beautiful pattern. Do not expect me to set exercises. Collect all the information you can about the appearance of Nature. That knowledge is knowing how to draw.

APPENDIX : Reprinted from *The Art and Craft of Drawing* . 149
How to arrange an experimental perspective apparatus. How to
use it. How to trace the Horizon Line experimentally. How to
find the Point of Sight. How to find the Distance Point. Vanishing Points. Parallel lines.

GLOSSARY 155

INDEX 161

LIST OF PLATES

A Cherry Tree . . . . *Coloured Frontispiece*

Photograph of Trees and a Bridge . . . *Face p.* 12

Photograph of the Cherry Tree. By G. L. Arlaud, Lyon . 18

Glass and Apples on a Table 26

After Dinner 27

'The Fisherman', by Claude Lorrain. Photograph by Mansell . 30

Six Plaquemines by Mou-hsi } From Gross's *Das Ostasiatische Tuschbild*,
Part of Drawing by Mou-hsi } by permission of the publisher, Bruno
Cassirer, Berlin . . 36 *and* 37

Photograph of a Chestnut Tree in Corsica. By G. L. Arlaud, Lyon 78

Photograph of the Acropolis, Athens. By Artists Illustrators, Ltd. 84

A Sketch by Paul Cézanne. By the courtesy of Sir Michael
Sadler 102

Drawing of the Chestnut Tree 104

Pine Trees. Photograph by G. L. Arlaud, Lyon . 110

A Stone Bridge in Corsica. Photograph by G. L. Arlaud, Lyon . 118

Sketch of Street in La Cavallerie 124

Photograph of Trees in a Field 128

A Cherry Tree 130

A Palm in Corsica. Photograph by G. L. Arlaud, Lyon . 131

A Group of Trees 133

PREFACE ... FOR THE 'OTHERS'

WHEN first the idea of writing this short book came to me, I meant it to be a book for children only; but when I began to work seriously on it, I also began to realize several things to which I had not paid sufficient attention before I began. Quite true that the great text of my sermon was from the beginning clear and evident to me: Drawing is a beautiful and intensely interesting thing, and so is the learning of it. It is not class-room drudgery—as, so often, it is made to be; it is nothing else than knowing how to see the beauties of construction and of effect in the natural universe. In a word: Learning to draw is learning to see.

Before I began to write I thought that it would be quite easy to explain this little by little to a juvenile audience. I still think that it is. But I now realize—and I believe that I am right in this—that this explanation must indeed be done 'little by little', must be backed up by the repetition of innumerable examples; examples that may be looked at with both eyes, felt, perhaps, with all ten fingers. The abstractions of the child are many, but they are not those of the philosopher and aesthete. The child's abstractions are his own affair; the realities of our grown-up life, which we lose no occasion of forcing upon him, will soon make an end of them, just as our grown-up drawing will make an end of his primitive art, with which (in spite of certain modern movements which it is not the place to examine here) our grown-up art has nothing, or so very very little, to do. His own abstractions he invents for himself; but when we want him to learn to understand ours, our grown-up abstractions, the difficulty begins.

.   .   .   .

The very existence of this book naturally raises a question which would not have been asked fifty or sixty years ago in Europe,[1] when naïve suggestiveness of untrammelled childlike invention had not yet been lauded, or at most had only been praised as a past thing executed by some primitive of Florence or Sienna. The child left to himself never draws from Nature, never studies in the way I suggest in these pages; he draws 'from his imagination'. It is undeniable that such drawings have a very definite aesthetic value. They contain, they depend on, much which lies at the base of the arts of primitive peoples. To this I have drawn attention in a chapter on Primitive Art written for Captain Rattray's book on *The Religion of Ashanti* (published by the Clarendon Press at the expense of the British Government). I have also examined primitive art in *The Art and Craft of Drawing*.[2] It is thus superfluous to do more than mention it here. The motive forces of primitive arts are practically in complete opposition to the programme set out in the following pages. Why have I not encouraged the child to continue, to perfect the naïvely imaginative art which is natural to him? Why have I directed him into completely different paths? Not, I beg you to believe, from want of meditation upon the subject.

The child's mind is moulded not only by hereditary tendencies, but by the environment in which he lives his

---

[1] I cannot here develop my reasons for adding the reservation of 'Europe'. I must, however, beg my reader to note that I have made it.

[2] Clarendon Press, 1927.

daily life. He has only one mind, not many ! When, at
the age of six, he does not deal consistently with logical
thought; when imagination and observed fact still com-
mingle casually in his mental act, and he cheerfully assures
you that he has just met a tiger in the back garden—one
kind of artistic impulse, the 'primitive', is natural to him—
his work on such lines will be to a certain extent 'good'
and interesting. But when you have slowly trained him
to more or less exact co-ordination between observation
and statement, you have at every step rendered *naïveté*
and primitivism more alien to his mind. Imaginative
primitive art becomes less and less the natural expression
of his mind. In these pages I have endeavoured to trace
the way by which he may arrive at being more or less
adept in the art which is an expression of the general mind-
form inevitably imposed upon him by his environment.
Yet I too lean towards regret that the naïve imaginings
of his early years can but be the ephemeral flowering of
an age so quickly past.

      .   .   .   .

Drawing is seeing. It may be no more difficult to
prove (?) the truth (?) of this aphorism than it is to prove
the truth (again imagine the question marks !) of any
other. But how are we to get our young gentleman or
young lady of eight or ten to follow our learned phrases ?
I fear the view out of the window, the casual dog, the
passing motor-car will prove far more interesting.
Still I am not without hope ; but success must be
pushed one degree farther off. I must begin by converting
to the doctrine a 'grown-up', who in turn shall administer
the gospel by very small doses at a time—small doses of
abstraction mixed with large doses of solid, tangible fact ;

of tree trunks which ARE round; of visible fact which CAN BE looked at with both eyes; of things which DO get smaller as they move off; of near trees which do seem darker in colour than more distant ones; of street foot-ways that do seem to meet in the distance; of horizontal building tops that do seem to slope downwards as they recede. And it is not once but many, many times that the child's naturally wandering attention must be called to these observations. Evidently such repetitions are not possible in book form. Did one even try to make them, no child would ever wade through the pages. I must fall back on the help of the 'grown-up' who in common with me desires (why do we?) to replace the inherent art of childhood by that complex thing of profound knowledge, of abstract aesthetic reasoning, of multiple manifestation, that art has become during the ages of man's habitation of the globe.

So I have restrained my first ambition to the minor one of—in the main—suggesting to the 'grown-up' what he or she shall say to the child, shall say many times to the child, shall say as often as possible to the child, and shall just as many times point out to the child about Nature herself—that is if so be that the 'grown-up' find any health in my argument.

At the same time I have employed the simplest language that I have found myself able to use. I have paid no attention at all to any kind of literary elegance. I have committed all possible crimes against style; have I not, time after time, finished a sentence with a preposition? I have done this in hopes of some children being willing to read part, at least, of the text, and also with the intention of furnishing as many phrases as possible ready-made to the intermediate 'grown-up'. I trust I shall not be pilloried for my crimes of *lèse-anglais,* nor for my repeated use of the first personal pronoun which always renders an explanation more vivid and easier for the child to seize. One tells him in a direct way what one wishes him to do.

I am conscious of my repetitions. They are made intentionally; a thing once said is rarely assimilated. It is by no means useless to repeat several times, varying slightly each time, both the language and the method of presenting an idea.

.   .   .   .

When I had written the greater part of these pages I handed them over to a young lady to read. 'But', said she, 'this is just what I have always been looking for! I have never been able to find any one who can explain to me what is the difference between a good picture and a bad one!' Of course! the thing had not occurred to me. When one describes the kind, the nature of the observation that, either consciously or sub-consciously, an artist of value makes with a view to enclosing its results in his picture, one has automatically defined the nature of the results, one has automatically defined a whole category of 'good' qualities of painting, in any case of good painting as it is generally understood and practised in contemporary Europe. I changed my title. I introduced explanations into the text; I pointed out in so many words that here were means of discriminating between good and bad pictures, at least in so far as drawing went. And drawing is the base of painting. Painting without shape is not painting. The loosest brush-work of Monet aims at suggesting *form,* though under the robe of colour, though behind the veiling of effect. Again, drawing is seeing; it is not the way in which the thing is done, but the way in which it is thought. Whether my intention be to represent the shape of an object by means of a clear-cut pencil out-line, or to represent it dimly shrouded in luminous and tinted mist, I must note the same facts concerning its solidity, its 'construction', its 'volumes', its 'planes', the 'suppleness' or the 'stability' of its kind ; I must submit all the observed facts to the perspective conventions on which we are agreed in modern Europe, to the codified conventions and to the admitted derogations from them. The observations which I make from Nature are in all their principal parts the same, whether I have in view one or other of those two extreme techniques. At the last moment I take up the pencil or I take up the brush, I either use my observations in a precise and clearly defined way, or mingled with 'effect', in a less precise, in a more suggestive way, allowing to charm of colour or to subtlety of light and shade a greater part in the work. Meditate upon this seeming paradox : The drawing is finished before ever the drawing is begun, or if it is not, it ought to be.

. . . .

But all this is much too difficult for children. Un-doubtedly. Art is a very difficult subject, and demands more years of study than any other. Let us go back to the accepted method for at least a few years until the child is old enough to understand better. Let us give him 'copies' to copy. Let us give him spheres to draw. Let us inculcate in him habits of tidiness by obliging him to rub out lines until they are of equal blackness all along, and quite sym-metrical on either side of the 'ornamental' (alas !) design. This will teach him perseverance and accuracy. It is an excellent training for him. One moment, please : what are we talking about ? moral training with a view to turning out good ratepayers by the dozen, each as like to the other as we can ; nine to four at the office, and so on ? Very sorry, but that is not precisely the subject taught here. You must have mistaken the address. We teach art here —or we try to do so. Whatever art may have been in hierarchic and ancient Egypt, in less ancient China—in both countries there was a firmly established aesthetic tradition which stretched over the centuries—two essentials of modern European art are individuality and innovation. True again, this innovation—modern Europe has decided it—must be based on natural observation. But that is precisely for what I am striving. A great proportion of modern art is emotional, why kill emotion in a dry-asdust class-room ? Probably on account of the ingrained British belief that emotion must neither be encouraged nor shown ; only a little cheap sentimentalism is to be allowed. How intensely uninteresting and monotonous British life is to those not perennially soaked in its apathy ! Can we not react against the materialism of the somnolent after-dinner arm-chair, the pipe which follows the plentiful plate of roast beef and potatoes ? Ah ! but the football and the cricket ! Be not deceived ; the materialism of twenty demands movement, the same materialism at forty demands its pipe and its very low and very easy chair. Art is a keen and nervous emotion which fixes itself upon beauty ; it is not somnolent, it is not apathetic, it is not tidy, it has no office hours. It is not concrete, though based on concrete phenomena. If you would teach art, encourage emotion caused by beauty, encourage enthusiasm ; do not suppress both as being in ' bad taste '.

That ugly class-room ! 'But there is beauty everywhere', some one cries. That may be so. However, be careful of the maxim. There may be degrees of beauty, degrees in the artistic values of different forms of beauty. Let us begin by encouraging children to enjoy the more obvious kinds, and leave to a later perception the estimate of those types of beauty that may be found in the sewer, to which Anatole France gently relegated *Zola* after the loss of his spectacles. No, give your child beautiful things to study and to draw from the start; for drawing is naught but the appreciation of beauty. What can one do to uproot the heinous fallacy that drawing is the copying of objects? Be careful, very careful, lest in the beginning you heap arid mountains of drudgery upon the nascent love of the beautiful that your child may show, upon a natural want which he may feel of creating a form of beauty of his own; lest you stifle, for years irreparably, a first fine delicate desire. The flower in its new blossoming is but a fragile thing. For seven years did my 'art masters' separate me from my future end in life. Thrice cursed be their names.

. . . .

But surely one must begin at the beginning and work one's way slowly upwards ! Did it ever occur to you that the beginning and the end of art, both, are beauty? That art and beauty are inseparable? That—let us say it at once—they are identical? How can we begin by the grammar of the subject, by that horrible dry invention of desiccated professors, of would-be creators who cannot create, of Rabelais's '*cervaux à bourlet, grabeleurs de corrections*', to whom he cries to get out of his sunlight, out from between him and the enduring source of life and beauty? How many of you would be condemned to eternal silence had you been forced to learn the grammar of your native tongue before you were allowed to speak it? By high fortune, still the nursemaid scoffs at the grammarian!

I, too, submitted to immobile years in the same unchanging class—the 'lower third' (!)—of Latin grammar; till one fine day (how came it to be permitted?) Horace thrust in :

Vides ut alta stet nive candidum Soracte.[1]

Long after, in subtle line and faintest violet tints, I drew the fair shape of that same Soracte; and, to-day, I am not wholly Latinless.

To the dust-heap with your grammars, with your plaster casts, with your schoolmaster's copies, with your tidy lines and your india-rubber! Rubbing out never yet made a Michelangelo who cut, unhesitatingly, Titans from the marble block. Learn from the first to see, to wonder at the rhythmic beauty of things, rise up and haste towards it, yield to its magnetism; what matter if you stumble on the way? Pick yourself up, stretch out your hands anew towards the ever unattainable—perfection of Beauty.

[1] See how supreme Soracte's high-snowed whiteness stands!

And pencil could not emulate
The beauty in this, how free, how fine
To fear almost! of the limit-line.

Robert Browning, *James Lee's Wife*
(VIII. Beside the Drawing Board).

*Look in the Glossary, p. 155, for any name which you do not
know, or for any word of which you do not know the meaning;
it will very likely be there.*

I

WHAT DRAWING IS

LEARNING to draw is learning to see. Many people think that drawing is a lot of mysterious ways of using a pencil, or a pen, or a piece of chalk, or a piece of charcoal so as to make a picture on a sheet of paper, a picture of things, a picture which shall be a nice tidy portrait of each one of them so that every one can see what it is meant to be. Now I don't mean to deny that there is not a wonderful lot of clever ways of using a pen in this way or in that, in order that the marks that we make on the paper may look 'like' leaves, look 'like' water, look 'like' a tea-pot, a cup and saucer, a sugar-basin. Unfortunately this is so. I say 'unfortunately', because the drawings done in this way are not generally worth very much, and have very little to do with art. If you know how to see, that is, if you know how to distinguish between the artistically important facts and those which are only of a less importance, you have only to scribble these facts down anyhow on a piece of paper and you will be surprised to find how 'like' your drawing is to what you have drawn it from, especially if you look at your drawing from a little way off. This is really the belief of a school of painters called Impressionists, because they painted the impressions they received from Nature, who worked much in this way about fifty years ago in France, and have been very much imitated since. If you work in that way you may call yourself an Impressionist too. But perhaps you don't believe what I have just said about scribbling shadows and things in anyhow. If so, the best thing I can do is to leave off writing and make just such a scribble, or just such a drawing, whichever it pleases you to call it.

Now don't you think you can scribble just about as badly as that (Fig. 1)? I haven't taken any kind of trouble with my pen ; I have just used it anyhow ; and although the result is not very good and very clever and all the rest of it, still I think you can see what the things are meant for. That's just the funny part of it : I scribble anyhow on a piece of paper and somehow or another my scribbles look like a tea-pot and a tea-cup and other things. Let us try to find out why.

The first thing I want to tell you is that when I left off writing just now I didn't begin to draw at once out of my head. I went and got a tea-pot, and a tea-cup, and all the rest, and set them out on the table in front of me. I have been drawing and painting and cutting stone into statues for the last thirty years ; all the same I don't start to make a scribble like this one without having the things them-selves in front of me, that is, if I want the scribble to be at all a good scribble. I should advise you too only to scribble in front of the things themselves. Just now I told you that learning to draw was learning to see ; if you've got nothing to look at you can't learn to see it! Perhaps the best thing to do will be for me to tell you just how I 'saw' this group of things arranged so as to make what we artists call a 'Still Life'.

FIG. 1. This is a very rough scribble from tea-things and a decanter. It is meant to show that it doesn't matter how you scribble the lines, if only you choose the right things to scribble down. Attention has been paid to the *importance* of certain things, and to the 'pattern'—which is really the same thing—but no attention has been paid at all to 'the way in which it has been done'.

First of all I noticed that the tea-pot was fat and round, and then I remembered that the window from which the light was coming was on my left hand, so all the shadows in the Still Life were on the right-hand side of the things and sloped a little away from me. When an object is solid, and not transparent, it stops some of the light that falls on it from going any farther, so one side of the object is darker than the other ; also a shadow falls on the table or the ground on the side away from the light. When we look at things, the best way we have of understanding that they are solid, that we can take hold of them if they are small enough, or that we can walk round them if they are bigger, is by noticing that one side is light and the other darker. If we want to make a drawing look like them, one of the best things we can do is to copy these shadows by making some parts of our paper darker than others, just in the places where the dark shadows come on the objects themselves. So when I noticed that the tea-pot was shaped like a ball, I at once noticed also that I saw its round shape mostly because it was darker just to the left of the bottom of the spout and also just over the spout. Moreover the feet of the tea-pot threw shadows on the table, and all the table under and to the right of the tea-pot was in shadow and so darker than the rest. I scribbled in these patches of shade at once, pretty well in their right places, but, as you can see, without taking much care about it. Then I did the same kind of thing when I came to the cup and saucer and the sugar-basin and the plate. All these things showed up against a dark background, against which the far edge of the table appeared light. When I looked at the glass decanter I saw that the edge of the table, which I saw *through* the glass, looked much higher up than the rest, and seemed to be curved. This is due to what scientific people call 'refraction'. You will notice that in my scribble I put these facts down, I mustn't say carefully, because my drawing is a very untidy one ; anyway, I put them down. If I didn't put them down

carefully I did one thing carefully : *I looked at the tea-pot
and the other things very carefully,* and that is just what

F<small>IG</small>. 2 shows how very often we need only put down the shapes of the
shadows in order to make people think that the things have really been drawn.
When shadows are clearly marked you should always take a great deal of
trouble over drawing them. You will generally find that the drawing looks
quite finished enough when you have done drawing the shadows. You notice
how there are *no outlines at all* in this diagram ; and that none of the objects
have been drawn as one would naturally think that they ought to be. The
shapes of the shadows are specially useful in modelling the front (ground part)
of the picture.

people don't do nearly enough when they are drawing.
People look much too much at the drawing, and not
nearly enough at the model. If they would do just the

opposite their work would be very much better. It isn't
what you do on the paper that matters, it's what you think
before you do it that is of so much importance. So long
as you choose the right thing to put down on the paper
it hardly matters a bit how you put it down; the great
difficulty is to choose the right thing; that's where all the
trouble comes in; that's what takes such a very long time
to learn. It's a very funny thing, but just what we are inclined to think the most important thing is nearly always
the least important. You would think that the edges of
a house are the most important to draw, and you want to
begin at once by drawing straight lines along the roof and
down the corners of the walls. But look at Figure 2.
I think you will see that it is meant to be a house and
a fence and so on. If you look carefully at it you will see
that I have drawn nothing but the shadows. The wooden
railings aren't drawn at all. You guess that they are there
on account of the shadows that they throw on the ground.
What is more, you see the shape of the ground; you see
that there is a ditch at the left of the picture; it is only
the shape of the shadow that makes you think there is
a ditch just behind the fence. Any reasonable person
would have thought that if we want to draw a fence and
a ditch we must draw a fence and a ditch, and that it
would not be any use at all only to draw the shadow of
a fence. But you see from this drawing that there are
a lot of things in art which don't happen at all as reasonable people would expect them to happen; and that here
the shadow of a fence is quite enough to *suggest* the existence of both a fence and a ditch. And there's the big

word let loose ! *Suggestion* is at the bottom of it all ! If
I do draw a tea-pot on a piece of paper, at the best of times
my drawing is not a real tea-pot ; I can only *suggest* a tea-
pot to you. What we have to do is to look at the model,
at the tea-pot, at the fence, and choose what will best
suggest their existences. There are lots of different ways
of suggesting a tea-pot. Many teachers will tell you to
draw a nice tidy line all round it, which will give you
a great deal of trouble, and will take a tremendous lot of
rubbing out and putting in again before you get it not too
crooked ; and I am afraid that you will get very tired of
that drawing and others like it before you get very far
on towards making a really good drawing. I don't want
you to get tired. Art is a most interesting subject ; we
ought to take a keen delight in exercising it, and we can
take this delight if we only set about doing it in the right
and interesting way. I don't mean to say that it does not
want a great deal of work to turn us into capable draughtsmen—it does ; it takes years and years ; still this work can
be most interesting and attractive. Why should it be
turned into an annoying drudgery of india-rubber and
tidy black lines, that refuse to get tidy however hard
we work at them ? And then one thing is sure to happen
if you use india-rubber and try to make tidy lines : before
long you will be looking at your drawing a great deal
more than you look at the model. Just try once if this
isn't true. A little way back I have said that drawing
is learning how to see things ; while you are looking at
your drawing you can't very well be learning how to see,
how to look at the model ! No, choose nice interesting

things to draw, and look at them, study them very carefully, notice how they are made, or how they have grown.
It is wonderful how interesting things get as soon as we
begin to pay attention to them. Until one begins one
would never think how interesting it is to find out what
a pretty pattern there is inside that little white flower
that we didn't even notice before : or how amusing it is
to see how the cabinet-maker arranged the joints of that
chair or table, or how the shoulder-blades of the cat stick
up in the air when she plants her fore-paws on the ground
in a certain way while she is squatting down. What
comes of all that kind of noticing is the sort of thing we
must treasure up if we mean to draw ; we should even go
on with our curiosity and understand all about the arrangement of the pistil, the stamens, the petals of the flower,
about the way in which the cat's shoulder-blades are
joined to the bones of her front legs, and even the more
we know about cabinet-making the better we shall draw
a chair or a table. Learning all about the shapes of things
is part of learning how to see them, and learning how to
see them is learning how to draw them. Your drawing
doesn't matter a little bit, *so don't be anxious about it, don't
rub out all the lines that aren't tidy.* Just make up your
mind what you mean to put down on the paper, and then
put it down as well as you can straight off. Perhaps it
won't be very well done to begin with; that doesn't matter ;
*when you have done some hundreds of drawings you will
find that they get better and better done as you go on.* So
don't use expensive drawing-paper; any thin wrapping-
paper will do; and instead of trying hard to correct a

wrong drawing, make another one all over again. Learning to correct bad drawings (or rather learning to tidy them up) is not learning to draw. *Learning to draw is learning to make a good drawing straight off.* Learning to draw is learning to see, learning to correct is not learning to see. And what is worse, we don't really learn to correct ; with all our rubbings out, we only learn to tidy up, which is not at all the same thing. A drawing is not necessarily good because it is untidy, but a drawing made by a beginner will probably be bad if it is tidy. There is only one real way to learn to draw : it is to look at the model, to examine it, to try to understand it, to try to decide as to what are the most important facts about the lights and shadows on it. When we have learnt to do this properly we have learnt how to draw.

. . . .

But let us return to my scribble that I made from the tea-things. I said something about the way in which the edge of the table appeared higher up and curved when seen through the glass of the decanter. If we want our drawing of a decanter to 'look like glass' we must carefully remark all sorts of facts of this kind, all sorts of reflections of shade and light which are often twisted out of the shape that they would naturally have if they were just ordinary reflections in a looking-glass. It is just these changes and twistings which will suggest in the drawing the shape of the decanter or the vase. It's not a bit of good your trying to imagine how these twistings will go and trying to draw them out of your head; you must look carefully at the vase, and put down what you see, not what you think you ought to see. What is the good of learning to draw if you know everything about that sort of thing to begin with ? If you do know all about it, well, you know how to draw. As for me, I am always surprised to find that such and such a reflection 'goes like that'; I should never have thought so. Nature always surprises us right to the end of a long life of study.

The shadow side of a round object is, of course, darker than the light side ; but most things reflect light ; indeed, it is by the light which they reflect that we see them. The table-cloth underneath and all round the tea-pot is white, so it reflects some light back into the shadow on the right-hand side of the tea-pot. You will see that I have noted this in my scribble by leaving the lower right-hand border of the tea-pot lighter than the rest of the shaded part. You should always look for these reflected lights ; they nearly always exist, and they help to suggest that the round shape goes on going round into the paper, that the object is really round. Although we are not conscious of it, we are really used to seeing this kind of reflection in the shadow every time we look at things ; so when we look at a drawing in which the reflection is noted, we feel comfortable about the business—we feel that everything is all right, that the tea-pot really is round. Ordinary people who can't draw don't notice that they see these reflections. Artists do notice that they see them. When I say we must learn to see, I mean that we must learn to notice all the details of what we see, learn to notice both that we *do* see and *what* we see. Then we shall be able to put down on the paper what we and everyone else really do see, though it isn't by any means everyone who understands that he does see in that way.

.   .   .   .

I have hardly used any outlines in my scribble. You can see in Figure 2 that outlines are not needful at all. Those I have used in Figure 1 are hardly worthy to be called outlines, they are so badly done. I might have done without them altogether as in Figure 2. In the cup in the front of the picture you will see that I have drawn no outline along its left side, because I did not feel that it was *important* enough to be put in. Why put in an outline between the part of the saucer that I have left white, and the part of the cup that is white too? We are, this time, making notes—very roughly scribbled notes, very care-lessly scribbled notes—of what strikes us first on looking at the tea-things. Now it is not the boundary between two white parts of our subject that strikes us as being very important; indeed we have to look very hard at our Still Life before we can see just where the boundary comes. If we were doing a very highly finished drawing of this Still Life we might have to notice exactly where the tea-cup ends and the saucer begins; but don't let us try to do a finished drawing yet, because a finished drawing is not a tidied up drawing, but a drawing which contains thousands and thousands of facts that we have noticed on the model, facts of appearance which we have put down carefully, one after the other, in the right order of *impor-tance*. Before we can do this with any hope of success we must have already made hundreds and hundreds of draw-ings, or it would be much better to say, we must have

Fig. 3 is meant to show with how few lines, if one chooses them rightly, quite a complicated subject can be represented. The drawing was begun by putting in the trunk of the middle tree, because the real subject of the picture is the three tree trunks, and that one is the most important because the path 'takes us' to it. The second thing put in was the right-hand trunk, which at once made a simple but incomplete balance. Then came the third trunk in order to get in the main subject: the three trunks. Then the horizontal lines of the bridge and the two dark accents under it were drawn; because they make an accent to which the eye 'goes' along the path. Then the lines representing the surface of the path; then the wriggly line along its side; then the lines which indicate the masses of plants and rushes on each side of the path. These help us to feel that we are 'going over them' and 'into' the picture. The marks at the top suggest the underside of the leaves, and so 'shut down' the picture, and make us feel that we are looking *under* the trees. Each thing noted is noted for a reason; it helps to explain the state of things.

FIG. 4 is a photograph of the subject from which the sketch was really done. In another drawing one might note the patch of light in front of the bridge, and that the foreground is in shadow, and, in short, pay less attention to line and more to light and shade. That is in part the artist's business and in part depends on the subject chosen. But an artist who wishes to work in line should not choose light-and-shade subjects. And vice versa. (Although the camera was placed where I sat, the opposite sketch looks different from this picture, because the lens took in a wider angle than I had dealt with.)

studied carefully and thoughtfully hundreds and hundreds of subjects hundreds and hundreds of times, for it is not so much the drawings which count as the attentive looking at Nature.

What do I mean by 'importance'? You have all of you seen quite finished pictures containing a great lot of detail ; you also know that quite a few lines, scribbles, or dots made with a pen or a pencil like those in Figure 3 suggest quite sufficiently the landscape reproduced in Figure 4. According to whether you make a drawing with lines, or with shading, or with both, the *important* facts that you notice first, and use first, will not be quite the same. Just now, when scribbling the tea-cup, I did not use a profile—between two white parts—which I should have used, probably, if I had been making a drawing in line. Although the important facts will not be *quite* the same always, many of them are. I cannot give you any rule for distinguishing in each case between the importance of one fact and the importance of another. Being able to judge this difference is knowing how to draw. We are learning how to judge this difference each time we study the model, each time we try to understand what we see, and then transfer what we see to the paper intelligently. You will understand better what I mean by 'importance' when you have finished reading this book. The greater part of it will really be only pointing out the most important facts in each example which I give you.

It always ought to be great fun to make a sketch or to paint a picture. You should always enjoy yourself while you are doing it. If you get bored over such work—or why shouldn't we call it play?—you may be sure that what you do won't be any good. I had great fun for half an hour painting the sketch which has been reproduced in colour as the frontispiece to this book. That's mainly why I asked to have it put in. I had been painting an almond tree in blossom all the afternoon, and wasn't particularly pleased with the result, so when the sun had got a little too far down in the sky, and the shadows weren't any longer in the right places, I packed up my easel and went a little farther along the path. Then I passed through a kind of court-yard in front of a group of houses built in stone and dating from about three hundred years ago. Opposite them is a great reservoir for washing clothes in. Through it runs ceaselessly the perfectly transparent water of a spring. But I didn't stop there. I went on into the open fields beyond, and as soon as I got past the houses and their gardens I turned round to look behind me. The sun was just going to drop behind the hill on my left, and everything was already turning golden in the evening light. All of a sudden I saw what I really wanted to paint! The bare February branches of a kind of willow tree, lit as they were by the evening sun, struck a vivid orange across the blue of the early spring Provençal sky. The orange and the blue! and then there was the yellow-green of the grass in the foreground. I got my easel up as quickly as I could and meant having a real bit of colour fun to make up for my

rather unsatisfactory painting afternoon. So I really
didn't care a bit what I did, so long as I did something
with blue and orange and yellow-green in it. At any rate
that was my first idea. But of course, in order to make
the colours 'tell', I had to have some dark accents, and
some blue and purple shadow tones. In this little book
I haven't been able to tell you anything about this making
colours 'tell', or making them 'luminous' or full of light.
I said quite a lot about that in *The Way to Sketch*, so it
is really not worth while repeating it here. But I didn't
want to write this book without saying anything at all
about how colour and drawing 'join up' and ' help' one
another. That is another reason why I asked to be
allowed to have a colour frontispiece. It is all very well
to put down the right colours on the paper or canvas ; that
alone would be a great point gained ; but if as well you
arrange them as a colour pattern with its light and dark
accents you will be surprised to find how much they are
improved. Then, if the colours themselves are gay, you
ought to arrange them in a gay kind of way, in order
to keep all your picture in the same kind of feeling. As
a matter of fact you are pretty certain to do that, because
if you are dealing with, copying, or inventing gay colour
you will be in a gay frame of mind ; and as you are
alternately inventing the tint and where to put it, you are
certain to be in the same state of mind while you are
inventing both. Of course if, on the contrary, you happen
to be sad—well, you'll invent sad colour and sad placing of
it. Sad colour may be very nice too, because sad colour
need not be 'bored' colour. But for the moment I don't

want to talk about either of them, because I am looking at
the sketch I made a year ago now, and remembering how
glad the colour was—it is nearly as glad this evening
at just the same time and on about the same day of the
month ; the evening sun is coming in at the open window
and casting greenish shadows on the paper, which is
all pale gold on the roller of the typewriter, shadows
which play about among the violet letters that I keep on
adding one after another, line after line.

Well, I started on my sketch, I remember, and thought
that as I meant having some fun I might just as well put
the sky in a much deeper blue than it really was ! Why
shouldn't I, if I felt like doing it ? Of course, if I made a
mess of it, that was my look-out.   But I thought that,
within reason, the stronger and bluer and (a little) greener
I made my sky the more brilliant the orange trunk and
branches would become, and they were really what I set
out to paint.   You should always—I have said so before—
be quite clear about *why* you are drawing or painting
anything, and all the time you are at work never forget
what that 'why' is.   Keep on coming back to it.   Let
everything call attention to it.   Let everything else only
be there in order to make that 'why' more of a 'why'
than ever.   My 'why' was making colour dance, so the
first thing I did was to put it on the paper in separate
brush-marks.   If I had painted the sky all over with
a tidy uniform tint, like painting a door, it wouldn't have
been half so dancy.   And then I wasn't going to be
serious and hard-working and tidy, and all sorts of proper
things like that ; I was just going to have some colour fun,

and as soon as I got tired of putting blue on the sky—well,
I'd leave off and put some orange on the tree trunk, or
some yellow-green on the grass, or feel quite determined
about things by placing a nice dark purple-brown shadow
accent somewhere or another where I felt at the moment
that the dancing rhythm wanted me to—to—to put my
foot down hard! You wouldn't believe what fun it is
taking colours off a palette and putting them on paper or
canvas in that way. Of course the sky, even here in the
south of France, ought not to be so dark a blue low down
near the horizon; but I wasn't trying to copy what I saw,
I was being very naughty and doing just what I liked.
And what I liked, my 'why' for the moment, was nice
blue blue and nice orange orange, and as long as they
made a pretty dancing pattern—well, I cared for nobody,
no, not I, and very likely nobody cared for me, although
I was a painter and didn't have a mill on the river Dee!
So I thought the pattern wanted some cream-white light
on the stone wall in about the middle of the picture. I put
it in. Then that made me think that I wanted to put
a little more cream-white on the distant house (it was
a house, though you might not guess it from the picture),
so I put that in. *I* didn't mind! But if you think I was
going to take the trouble to make it quite clear that it was
a house by making an outline all round it and carefully
painting my cream-white colour up to that outline, you're
very much mistaken. What did it matter to me whether
you understood that it was a house or not? I didn't care
about what you thought, I was enjoying myself; so when,
after two or three brush-strokes of cream-white, I got

tired of that and wanted to do something else, I *did* do
something else.   So long as my two patches of white
attracted attention to the middle of my pattern and
balanced up its rhythm, that was all *I* wanted, so I let it
go at that.   You can take them for copies of *The Times*
newspaper or two polar bears out for a walk.   *I* don't
mind.   *I* was only having some fun with colour.   Only
we can't even have fun *really* without having fun *properly*.
When you play blind-man's-buff you've got to pay some
attention to the rules of the game, or else you'll all quarrel
and won't have a good time at all.   So it's no good putting
any old colour on the paper in any old way: you'll only
make a mess and get tired of it very soon.   When you put
your colour on you must put it on according to the rules
of the game—of the game of rhythm and balance.
Oh, it doesn't really matter a bit if you balance with
a polar bear or *The Times*, but *you must balance* or you
won't have any real fun.   You see in this picture, as soon
as I got my two bits of white down I was obliged to put in
that bit of buff-coloured wall over on the left to make a
sort of die-away balance for them.   Cover it up with your
finger and see how uncomfortable the want of it makes
you feel.   And being uncomfortable isn't having fun.

I got Monsieur Arlaud, who was here a few days ago, to
take a photograph of the place (Fig. 5), in order to show you
a little what it really looked like; but I see that he has taken
it just a bit too much to the right, so you don't see that
light buff piece of wall (which is in a straight line with the
white stone wall in the middle of the picture), you only
see the dark part of the wall in shadow, the part I have

Fig. 5

Photograph by G. L. Arlaud, Lyon

painted bright ultramarine blue (for fun !) in the picture. Then the photograph was taken just a few minutes later than the moment at which I painted the foreground, because the two shadows of the trees outside the picture are now lying over it—or perhaps I left them out because I wanted to keep all the foreground as far as possible bright yellow-green : I forget. Don't forget (I didn't) that I was doing just what I liked. In the pattern that Monsieur Arlaud's picture makes, the cherry tree in the foreground is the most important thing—the thing we look at. He was obliged to make it so. The camera won't leave things out (sometimes, if you do photography yourself, you may have found that it leaves everything out altogether, but that is not what I mean !); but I left out just what I wished as I was only amusing myself, so amongst other things I left out most of the cherry tree—as well as leaving out altogether the tree between it and the orange trunk. Monsieur Arlaud has felt obliged to take his picture a little more to the right than I did, because the camera made the cherry tree the most important thing in the picture and he felt that it wouldn't do to have the most important thing too far over to the right. What catches the eye in my little joke is the patch of white wall, so *I* let the cherry tree go in order not to have two points of interest in the picture.

You see a sketch is just a happy rhythmic balance, that and nothing more. A photograph is a complete picture, or I would rather say a complete copy of Nature ; so although both, to be at all satisfactory, must obey the rules of the game of balance, still they need not be balanced in exactly the same way. If I had finished my picture I might have been obliged to come to much the same kind of balance as that of Monsieur Arlaud's picture, but as I was leaving out whatever I liked, and even moving things about as I liked, I was able to use quite a different balance from his. In a sketch you put in just what is wanted to make it balance. Why should you be bothered to put in more? for all sketching is fun. Just go over my sketch and cover up with your finger the dark or light patches on it, one after another. I think you will in each case want each patch back again, just as I wanted to put it there. That's the real way to make a sketch, putting things on the paper because you want them to make a balance. The wrong way to go about the work is to put in all the windows of a house because they are there; and when you have begun to draw a window, to go on drawing it until it is quite done, just as if it were a sum in arithmetic or a Latin exercise. No, you should dance about all over the place just where you want to, and then your sketch will probably be as lively and interesting as you felt the game to be when you were playing it.

You may say that I began by saying that my 'why' was the orange branches and the blue sky, and that afterwards I said that the 'point of interest' was the white wall. This is not really a contradiction. The orange branches and the blue sky were a 'colour idea', but to 'publish' that idea satisfactorily I had to fit it out with a pattern, and the pattern I chose was the one in which the interest is fixed on the white patch. But I didn't forget my first idea for a single instant. All the tints of my pattern are decided by my blue-and-orange colour idea.   It is because of that idea that my dark accents are just such a dark purple, that my blue shadows are just such a vivid blue.   All that makes up a colour rhythm in which the form rhythm is carried out.   The orange branches and the blue sky decided once for all the ' key of colour ' in which I was going to paint my pattern.   Those were the rules which I kept to while playing my little game, having my little joke all to myself.   So you see a little bit how colour rhythm and pattern rhythm, about which I have bothered you so much in this book, may be made to join up and work together.

II

WHAT TO DRAW

WHAT shall we draw? That matters a very great deal, for reasons some of which I shall find very difficult to explain to you before you know a lot more about the subject. One of the reasons (and perhaps, after all, it is the most important) I am sure you will understand at once. When I was a little boy of twelve I attended the drawing class at school on Wednesday afternoons. I was given a horrible print of a scrolly kind of thing that was supposed to be an ornamental design. I was made to draw a 'free-hand' straight line down the middle of the paper, and I was told to copy faithfully the hideous curves of the 'design' with the tidiest possible line. I was supposed to get both sides of the drawing exactly alike. I still do not understand what I was supposed to learn by so doing. So far as I remember I took the better part of the term over this task, which was just as uninteresting, and much less useful, than Latin grammar exercises. Either at the end of the first term, or at any rate at the end of the second, I was so disgusted with the whole business that I asked my father to let me leave off drawing and have a half-holiday instead. I said to myself: 'If that's drawing, I don't ever want to have any more to do with it!' and I didn't until I was nearly twenty. I studied science instead, chemistry and physics. My drawing (!) masters were responsible for losing me seven years of

study of my future profession. When I was older I found
out for myself that that wasn't drawing at all, in fact that
it had nothing whatever to do with drawing. I found out
that Turner understood drawing to be studying Nature,
and not copying the 'free-hand copy' invented by some
drawing-master. Drawing is not copying, it is seeing
Nature.

Moreover, one of the things that beginners (and even
most of those who are not beginners) succeed least in is
'seeing solidly'. Leonardo da Vinci, the great Italian
painter who lived during the fifteenth century, told us in
his writings that the aim of painting is to represent bodies
in relief on a flat surface. This may not be quite all the
story, but for the moment it will do for us. Now if you
copy a flat drawing from a flat printed 'copy' you won't
learn anything at all about 'seeing solidly'. It is always
easy enough to 'draw flat'; the difficulty is to 'draw
solidly', to make the person who looks at the drawing
feel that the tea-pot is really round, is really in relief, is
really 'natural', has thickness as well as width on the
paper, has thickness *into* the paper. You remember that
the first thing that I noticed on looking at the tea-pot was
the shadow side of it, which was nothing else but the
result of the *thickness through* of the tea-pot. And I scribbled that shadow down as being most important. When
you draw anything, especially when you draw any group
of things, make up your mind just how the things are
arranged on the ground or on the table; you should be
quite ready to make what is called a ground-plan of what
you are drawing, a plan like Figure 6, which is one of the

arrangement of the tea-things in Figure 1. This is the kind of thing over which you cannot take too many pains, in order to understand all you possibly can about what you are drawing. You must never *think* carelessly, however carelessly you scribble down the result of your thought. Besides, if you think a moment, you will understand that the more you have thought out what you are going to do, the less carelessly you will really do it, even though you do not pay much attention to the actual doing of it.

But this is not the chief reason for not choosing one of these terrible copy-book 'vases' or 'ornamental' (?) designs over which to tire yourself out; the chief reason is that they are not a little bit interesting or amusing to draw. When I begin to feel annoyed, or tired, or disinterested in what I am painting, I leave off at once. Art which brings no joy or satisfaction to the worker, while he is working, is not art. It may be some kind of a trade, or it may be . . . I am sure I don't know what; but I do know that it isn't art. I know that when I try to draw something that does not interest me very much, I only do bad work. The more the subject interests me, and the more it makes me forget my surroundings and everything else, the better will be my drawing. So, above everything, let us only choose things which interest us to draw. Very often we have a particular liking for something or another, we take more interest in that thing than in anything else. I don't think I should be far wrong in advising you, as often as not, to exercise yourself in drawing things which interest you already . . . always supposing that they are not too difficult or too complicated.

But most people like looking at big views, and many beginners at sketching sit down cheerfully to try to paint such views. This is pretty certain to lead to failure. Why? Because it requires a great deal of knowledge to reduce

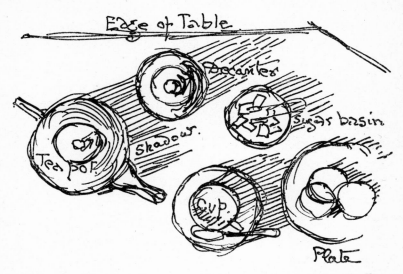

Fɪɢ. 6 is a plan of the arrangement of the tea-things scribbled in Figure 1. You should never draw anything without being quite certain just how the parts of it are placed on the table or on the ground. You should always take the trouble to decide just how far one object is behind the other. If you do, the result will look right in your drawing. Everything that you know about what you are drawing comes out in your work. A really good drawing is full of all kinds of knowledge.

all the details of thousands and thousands of trees, of perhaps hundreds of fields and hedges, of perhaps a great many houses, to a few simple *important* facts of shadow or light or line. So while telling you only to draw things which interest you, I will add that you will be very wise if you only draw *very simple* objects which interest you to

begin with. Anyway, never make yourself draw something which it does not interest you to draw at all. If one
simple thing does not interest you, choose another which
does. If nothing interests you at all, I think you had better
not try to draw; you will be much better employed in
learning something else, or even in going for a ride on
a bicycle or playing at hockey or some other game. Later
on in this book I am going to speak of many things about
which you have probably never thought, but when they
are once pointed out they make a lot of things interesting, which you would never have even noticed before, far
from being interested in them. So I hope to be able
to interest you in simpler things than perhaps a corner
of your garden; though you may like it very much, and
may be very interested in it, because, perhaps, you have
gardened there yourself. It would probably neither be a
good subject for you to begin on, nor ever make a good
picture.

Yes, quite so; not by any means everything will make
a good picture, not by any means everything which is
agreeable to look at can be drawn with success. The
people who set me to copy my fearful ornaments told me
to put them in the middle of the paper (tidily of course),
and there was an end of the matter—and not even a beginning of art. Now it is not at all an easy thing to be an
artist, and though some of us are born with the talent
which may in time enable us to become artists, still it is
only at the expense of a great deal of hard work (by which
I do not mean disagreeable work) that we can arrive at

FIG. 7. This is the reproduction of a sketch I made years ago at table. I have reproduced it to show how one can make an interesting pattern out of the most unexpected things, and how interesting an unexpected point of view and general arrangement becomes. You should compare this sketch (and the following one) with the diagrams which I have been obliged to make for this book. In this sketch I was an artist working with no afterthought; in the others I was doing what I thought I ought to do in order to show things and make nice blocks. You see how much better and freer and more interesting these two sketches are. They are done in colour, with lines drawn on wet paper with an ordinary copying pencil.

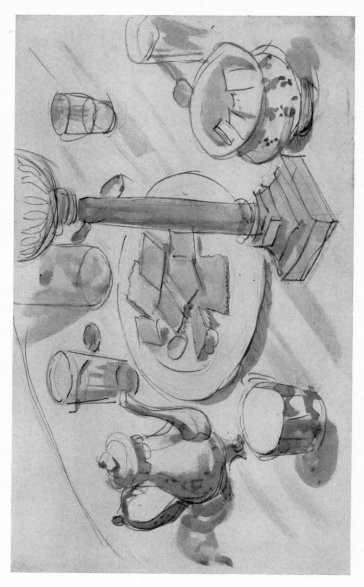

FIG. 8. The same remarks apply as to Fig. 7. Notice the decorative cutting of the plate of biscuits by the upright lamp-stand. This drawing is done in pen-lines and slight colour. You see how you should always be on the look-out for 'subjects' in the most unexpected places, and always be studying pattern-making, and values and things, even at table; where, by the by, you can often find most happy arrangements of elegant shape and colour in the flowers and fruit and dinner service in general, even though the things in themselves may not be very valuable. In both these sketches the things themselves are very ordinary, yet the sketches, especially in colour, are not at all disagreeable. In both these sketches, as I was sitting at table myself, the Horizon Line is far above the top of the paper, at the height of my eyes, of course.

painting really good pictures. As it takes such a lot of training to be an artist, I want you to begin to try to be one right from the very start.

Seeing what will make a good picture is perhaps the most difficult part of painting. I have no better advice to give you than to begin as soon as you can to find out as much as you can about what makes a good picture and what does not make one at all. About this I can give you some rules, though there are so many sides to art that it will be very easy for some clever person to find that I have left something out, or that what I say is not always strictly true. I must ask any such clever person to consult my other books; this one is not meant for him or for her: it is meant to direct the first steps of young people who, later on, may become, in their turn, very clever, but who are not so yet. For them I prefer simplifying things as much as possible, even if here and there I am obliged to say something which is not always true in what concerns it may be China, or ancient Greece, or the cubists.

Well, putting decorative work out of the question (and I am not talking about that at all in this book), I think we can safely begin on the rule : Don't put anything of particular interest exactly in the middle of the paper. Now by this I mean : If you are drawing a tea-pot and cup and saucer, take care that neither the tea-pot nor the cup and saucer are in the middle of the paper. I think this will be quite clear if we compare Figure 9 with Figure 10. Figure 10 makes a much more agreeable picture than Figure 9. Figure 9 is much more tidy but much less interesting, much less suggestive of all sorts of things, such as the tea-things having been left like that by two people who have been having an interesting conversation while they were drinking their tea, and so on. There is at once a suggestion of what artists call 'intimity' in such a picture ; but in Figure 9 this suggestion is quite wanting. You must never forget that the aim of drawing is not only the reproduction of things, but also, and much more so,

FIG. 9 shows how much less *interesting* a 'composition' is when we put the principal object right in the middle of the picture. It is true that the pattern is balanced; but it is balanced in too simple a way, just one thing on one side and a similar thing on the other. Any one can invent that ; it is not a matter of being an artist. This kind of quite 'even' composition is often useful in decoration, when the decoration is not the most important thing and, consequently, we do not wish to attract too much attention to it.

the suggestion of all sorts of ideas. Drawing is an art, and so are poetry and music. All three are capable of *suggesting* the same kind of ideas. People, in England especially, too often think that drawing means copying, making a portrait of something, and that is all. They are quite willing to admit the suggestiveness of music or of poetry, but they will not admit that an artist can use a line just as a musician can use a note of music. But this is too difficult for you to understand yet; all the same I want to say it to you at once, then as you go on you will gradually understand what I mean.

If we don't put the tree or the tea-pot—or whatever else may be the principal object that we are drawing—in the middle of the picture, where shall we put it? Before we can in any way answer this question, we must recognize

FIG. 10 is an unevenly balanced arrangement, an unevenly balanced pattern made from the same objects. We feel at once that the things may have been left like that by two people who were taking tea together, and who were talking about different things. A human interest is suggested, and art is mostly suggestion.

that anything which is suitable for making a picture from is never quite symmetrical, that is to say, both sides of it are not alike. Still more, we don't make pictures out of single objects. What we do, then, is to make up a sort of balance between big objects and little objects, putting more little things on one side to balance a big thing on the other. You can quite easily see that there are any number of ways of making up this kind of balance, so I really can't give you any hard and fast rule about 'composing a picture', as it is called. I can only give

you some examples; though I can give you this general
rule : *Always think of this balance ; study it in every picture
that you come across; try to find out whether the balance,
either in your own drawings or in other pictures, really
seems satisfactory to you.* The best way to learn something
about this balance is to look at pictures by great masters,
and to make scribbles of what is rather badly called their
' composition '.

.   .   .   .

The first example of composition that I have chosen is
a pen and wash drawing by Claude Lorrain, a great
French landscape painter who lived in the seventeenth
century. The original drawing is in the British Museum
Print Room, and has, moreover, been reproduced already
in the little series of *Drawings by Old Masters*, published
by Gowans & Co. I should advise you to buy this little
book, the volume specially given up to Claude's drawings,
and to study them very carefully. They are a very remarkable and instructive collection of picture compositions.

Figure 11 is the drawing itself, called ' The Fisherman ',
and Figure 12 is a scribble I have just made from it, the
kind of scribble that I should advise you to make as often
as you get the chance. The first thing we notice is that
the most *important* thing here is the group of trees. You
see at once that it is not quite in the middle of the picture,
although it very nearly is. But in a picture we must not
only consider the real things themselves, because a picture
is a pattern of darks and lights before all else, not so very
different, after all, from the design of a wall-paper or
a piece of embroidery. The dark shadow B is a thing

FIG. 11. This is a reproduction of one of the drawings by Claude Lorrain, called 'The Fisherman'. You should notice that it is not at all tidily done; it is really done in a quick scribbly fashion. Only Claude knew just what he was about and chose the right things to scribble. Why he chose the more important of the things is explained by Figures 12, 13, 14, and 17.

which counts very much in the pattern, so that really
brings our 'principal mass' A—as we call the trees in
this picture—very much over to the left indeed. In order
to counterbalance this lop-sidedness what has Claude
done? He has made the right-hand bottom corner C

Fig. 12 shows all the most important parts of the 'pattern' of Figure 11.

very dark indeed. These three things, the group of trees,
the shadow, and the dark in the front of the picture, already
make quite a satisfactory pattern in the frame (Fig. 13),
but they are not enough to make a picture. They are the
three most *important* facts concerning the *composition*.
After them come the less *important* facts that I have
added to my third scribble (Fig. 14). If we look again
at Figure 13, we shall feel that the group of trees A does

not seem to be properly 'held up'; Claude felt this too, so he put the dark mass D (Fig. 14) immediately under-neath the trees. You should always try to make your pattern in a picture—your 'composition' people usually say—look properly set down and built up. I shall have more to say about this later on, when we are talking about

Fɪɢ. 13 is another rough scribble, done anyhow, to show the three most important facts of the pattern : A, the group of trees, which the picture is really about, and which is not exactly in the middle, though near it. B, the shadow which the trees throw, and which has the effect of pulling them more than ever out of the middle of the picture. C, the dark mass in the foreground, which begins to build up the rest of the pattern.

drawing. Now that we have got as far as D, our scribbles are beginning to fill up the paper nearly enough, *as far as concerns the principal and secondary masses.* You should always take care not to overcrowd a picture. That is why,

at any rate for a long time yet, you should not try to draw
a corner of the garden nor a big view; you will be almost
certain to get too many things, too many bushes and
flowers and so on into it. Or, if you don't, you won't

FIG. 14 shows how the dark mass D has been added to 'hold up'
the trees, which seemed to 'float about' too much in Figure 13.
They didn't seem to 'belong to anything'.

know how to simplify properly, and your masses of flowers
and things won't look like anything at all.

Here I may as well give you another piece of advice.
A little way back I told you not to draw anything which
did not interest you; I told you only to draw things
which you found interesting. *But I did not tell you to draw
ANYTHING that you found interesting.* Things may

interest us for all sorts of reasons ; for example, they may interest us to collect, like stamps ; they may interest us in a scientific way. When I was about eleven I was very interested in geology ; I read lots of books on geology, I made collections of rocks and minerals every time I went away for my holidays, and I spent a considerable part of my time in South Kensington Museum. That is one way of being interested in things. But with that way we are not concerned for the moment. For the moment *the only way in which things should interest us is on account of some kind of pattern which we can make out of them when we draw them on a sheet of paper.* I had first written 'when we draw them on paper', but no sooner had I finished writing the word 'paper' than I said to myself : 'That is not all the story,' and as quickly as I could I put in the words 'a sheet of'. Why I did so I will explain to you a little farther on. If I had been able to, I should very likely have recommended myself, at the time when I was interested in geology, to make drawings of minerals and of stones, and better still, perhaps of quarries or of mountains, in which one could easily see and study all sorts of facts connected with the stratification of sedi-mentary rocks, or with the weathering of volcanic rocks, and so on. I should certainly have recommended myself to make drawings of the wonderful patterns that the skeletons of pterodactyls or plesiosauri have left imprinted between the strata of the secondary rocks. And how much more intelligent it would have been for my drawing-masters to have set me to draw the spiral of a fossil ammonite than to have put in front of me their stupid, tasteless, curly copies. It is never a mistake to draw things which interest us, *if such things lend themselves to the making of patterns.* You may be very interested indeed in your collection of postage stamps, but I should hardly recommend you to sit down and draw nothing but postage stamps ; indeed, in this case I should not recommend you to draw them at all, because what you would be doing there would simply be copying what are usually very bad designs : I would almost as soon send you to copy the horrible curly ornaments. So the interest which you may take in postage stamps is not one which is very useful to us at the present moment. Indeed, although I recommend you to make rough scribbles from Claude's pictures, from Titian's pictures, from Rembrandt, from Jean-François Millet, from Manet, from Cézanne, with a view to 'learning composition', I never advise you to *copy* even the works of great masters. *Always draw from solid objects, and always try to make out of them a picture or pattern (which is the same thing) of your own invention.* Although you may *learn* 'composition' from Turner, or Claude, or Michelangelo, or from Mou-hsi (Fig. 15)—a great Chinese painter who lived in about 1250 A. D.—never copy it from any of them ; always invent it for yourself anew. This is, I am inclined to think, the most difficult part of art, so you cannot begin to take pains with it too soon. Later on I will suggest some experiments that you may make yourself in order to exercise yourself in it.

.   .   .   .

Well, let us go back to our scribbles from the Claude drawing, which we have nearly forgotten all about. I think

F 2

DESCRIPTION OF FIGURE 15

These six plaquemines were drawn by the great Chinese artist Mou-hsi in about 1250. You see that even one of the greatest artists did not think that half a dozen fruits were not worth drawing, and he has made a masterpiece of them. Perhaps you think it is easy to do something like this. Well, I can tell you that nothing is more difficult ; this is the reduction of all art to its most simple form. Notice how solid they are. Notice how well 'set down' the composition is ; how the fruits seem to be resting on the surface, *which is not drawn at all*, and yet which we feel to be there. Notice how the top of the paper does not seem to be empty as it does in the photograph, Figure 36, in spite of the fruits being down at the bottom of the paper. This is because the pattern is exquisitely arranged with regard to the shape of the paper ; whereas in the case of the photograph none of that kind of balance is studied. Put your finger over the foremost fruit and notice how empty and uninteresting the rest seems to be at once. Note the cunning way in which the black fruit is just at an 'interesting' place in the paper, and how the three grey fruits, so to speak, 'shade off' from it, finishing up by the two white ones. This makes us feel that the fruits are not 'all alone' on the paper, because we gradually 'get away' so gently from the dark black fruit which first attracts the eye. Then notice how very ingenious is the spacing between the fruits. This is, of course, very important in the pattern. Some just overlap, some just touch, others have carefully considered spaces between them. Mou-hsi has given himself no chance of making a mistake which should not be seen. That is why the great critics of the East admire such pictures as this so much. All the difficulties of art are observed and vanquished in such a drawing. One might write a book about it alone. You may also judge your progress in understanding of art by the increasing number of successes which you see in this drawing.

FIG. 15. Six Plaquemines by Mou-hsi (about A.D. 1250)

FIG. 16. Lower part only of a painting by Mou-hsi (about A.D. 1250)

37

DESCRIPTION OF FIGURE 16

This is another drawing by Mou-hsi. This time it is only a part of a bigger drawing; there is a wild goose higher up. So the pattern is not altogether his. I want you to notice with what astonishing certainty he has put down the half-dozen brush-marks which draw the stem and leaves. I have said elsewhere that a drawing must be done in your mind before you begin it on the paper. Here Mou-hsi knew *exactly* what he was going to do before he began; and he did not use any india-rubber, nor 'try if it would do like that'! In the middle leaf look how astonishingly he has drawn the double twist by pressing more or less on the brush, and by finishing the end of the brush-mark just as it ought to be. You can never begin to hope to arrive at this amazing mastery, but it does no harm to study it. Look how decorative are the dots at the bottom left-hand corner *as they are placed in relation to the leaves.* He has concentrated all the difficulties and conquered them with just a few strokes of the brush.

we had just made up our minds that the 'principal and secondary masses' would 'do'; but somehow or other, even allowing for the difference between the carelessness of my scribble and the masterly drawing of Claude, a great deal of the 'charm', of the 'attractiveness', of the 'completeness' of Claude's pattern still seems to be wanting in our scribble. We have still left out something very important. We have placed our masses properly on the paper, but we have forgotten to join them together by what are called 'rhythmic movements of form'. Perhaps the best way to explain what these words may mean will be to remind you of what I said just now, that a painter or a draughtsman can use his line just as a musician uses his notes. You all feel, when you sing or whistle a tune, that one note seems to come 'naturally' after another to make a 'rhythm'. When you draw a curved line, one part of the line should come 'naturally' after another, just as the notes of music come 'naturally' after one another. There are all sorts of ways of 'coming after' naturally, so there are all sorts of tunes, and all sorts of curved lines. Being a musical composer or being a draughtsman is knowing how to arrange notes of music or bits of line so that they should seem to come naturally after one another. Or if I may put it into more learned language : *the base of all art is the knowledge of the use of rhythmic sequence*. There! I have written it down; I don't for a moment expect you to understand what I mean. But I must have my little joke once in a way! Claude placed his main masses with one kind of rhythm, with one kind of 'coming naturally after' in view, but he joined them together with another kind, with curved lines. Let us put in the most *important* of these curved lines—these rhythmic movements of form—in Figure 17. How much more satisfactory our scribble becomes at once! How very much more like

Fig. 17. In Figure 14 the things still seemed rather separated from one another. They wanted 'joining up'. So Claude put in the curved lines E, F, G, which wind in and out among the other things and lace them all together. These curved lines also 'take us away' into the 'middle distance' and into the 'distance'. (From B to G would be called the middle distance, and from G to the horizon, the distance.) Also in this figure the pattern has been completed by the horizon and the mountains on each side. They are on each side because the pattern or composition is of a 'central' kind, that is, fairly central though not quite.

the original drawing! I want you specially to notice that the lines E and F not only curve round together, but that they meet and only form one 'movement' at the bridge, G, and that it seems quite 'natural' to go on from their curves to the Horizon Line, H (Fig. 12), along which we 'come back' from left to right. In following the river we have crossed the picture in front of the trees. Then we have re-crossed the picture behind the trees in going to the bridge. Then we have once more crossed the picture behind the trees when we 'come back', from left to right along the Horizon Line. The effect of this continual crossing and re-crossing of the picture by *important* lines is to 'bring it all together', to make it all into one picture. That is why Claude drew that view from that particular point, and from no other. That is why it is not every view that we come across, or every corner of the garden, that is suitable for making a picture from. For : *A picture must be one thing ; all its parts must be satisfactorily joined up somehow or another with all the others.* It is just this 'joining up' which is the pattern. If you don't see any evident way of joining up all the parts of what you are looking at, don't try to draw it. If it happens to be a 'Still Life', add a piece of drapery, move one of the things till it is slightly behind another, until you see your way to joining things up properly so that the 'joining up' makes a pretty and agreeable pattern on your sheet of paper.

Finally, to complete his 'composition', Claude has added some distant hills. As this composition is balanced about a fairly central point, Claude has put some distant hills on the right and some on the left. In the drawing on the opposite page of Gowans's little book the point is not at all in the middle, but somewhere in the lighter tree trunk in the foreground ; but notice how all the forms lean over towards the left, taking all the 'weight' of the pattern over that way, and leaving very little to the right of the picture. The right-hand part of the picture is quite like the long arm of a Roman balance : very little weight on that side manages to *balance* quite a lot of weight on the other. This idea of balance has a tremendous lot to do with pattern-making. I shall often use the word 'balance' in this book. Notice in this last drawing how the line of the river again crosses the picture, and runs *between* the two trees. Also notice how we can 'get' quite easily up from the river bank by the line just in front of the palings on the extreme left, and back along the top of the down in the distance, this time *behind* the big tree. Hide with your finger—or better with a little bit of paper—the little tree on the right, and notice how important it is in making you feel 'satisfied' with the balance of the drawing. It is a little 'weight', but it is some way out along the arm of the balance, so it counts quite a lot. Here we have another example of, first, how the big masses are 'balanced' against one another in a picture pattern ; and secondly, how 'rhythmically arranged' lines, or curved sweeping lines—if the other words frighten you—run about among the big masses or weights, in order to join all the pattern up together in an agreeable way.

    .   .   .   .

But perhaps you are saying : 'All that is very well, only I don't want to learn how to make pictures : at any rate, I don't want to learn that yet. I want to learn to draw. I wish he would begin to teach me how to draw, instead of going on talking about Claude's composition

and all sorts of other things.' Although you may not yet
understand quite why it is so, I must ask you to believe
that I am really taking the shortest cut to teaching you
how to draw. I only wish some one had pointed it out to
me years ago—it would have saved me a lot of wasted
time. Let us go back to my first scribble (Fig. 1) or, if
you like, to any of the scribbles I have made from the
Claude drawing. Take any one line in one of these
scribbles and look carefully at it. There is nothing at all
wonderful about it ; any one could do it. How is it that
such a line manages to have anything at all to do with
drawing? Look at Figure 17, look specially at the line E.
Imagine it put anywhere else on the paper except just
where I have put it. Where I have put it on the paper
it becomes a part of the pattern, and also we easily understand it to be meant to be the river bank. Anywhere else
on the paper it wouldn't be a part of the pattern, and it
wouldn't mean anything at all. NOW do you see why in
the first place I have been doing such very bad scribbles
up to now, and why I have been talking such a lot about
pattern? *The worth of a line depends on its place on the
sheet of paper.* The most unskilful line in the RIGHT
place becomes a good line ; the most skilful line in the
WRONG place is a bad line. And the *right* place on the
paper is the *right* place in the pattern. The wrong place on
the paper is the place in which the line does not fit into
the pattern. If we are to fit a line into a pattern we must
have a pattern to fit it into. That is why I am talking
such a lot about pattern-making before I ask you to draw
a single line. If my old drawing-masters were to rise up

and say : ' But we were trying to teach you pattern-making when we made you draw your copies !' I should at once reply : ' If you had called my attention to the first-class patterns by Claude, by Douros, by Wou Tao-tseu, I should have been grateful to you ; instead, you not only set in front of me a piece of ornament (?) hideous in itself, but you completely stupefied me by making me rub out lines interminably, while I was made to endeavour to produce a dead mechanical piece of hard and fast tidiness. *Never study any works of art but those of the very greatest masters ;* their work is the simplest ; that is one of the chief reasons why they *are* great.   Don't believe any one who tells you that you are not old enough to understand great pictures yet. Go up to the pictures, look at them as I have been telling you to do, make scribbles of their main compositional facts, and when you have done that a few times I shouldn't be a bit surprised if you understand more about them than the people do who tell you that you can't understand them yet.   And about that tidy line question.   Look at the Claude drawings : are the lines tidy ? Even the lines of some of those very perfect Leonardo da Vinci silverpoint drawings are nothing like as tidy as the lines my masters wanted me to make. I suppose I ought to do things better than Leonardo did ; somehow or another, to-day, I shouldn't a bit mind doing them as well as he did : we'll see about doing them better afterwards.   Whatever you do, don't begin by trying to copy his faultless lines (I don't know whether my drawing-masters would have called them 'faultless'—I do) ; wait until you know as much about it all as he did.   Otherwise your line will be tidiness and not art, art as his was. In different places in this book I will tell you more about lines depending on how they are placed and used in a drawing.

．　　　．　　　．　　　．

Why, some little way back, did I write 'on *a sheet of paper*' instead of simply: 'draw them on paper'? Because the edges of the sheet of paper are very important. It won't do to put our drawing anywhere on the paper. The edges of our pattern are quite an important affair in the pattern. The best pattern placed all awry on the paper won't look nice, and whether we put the chief point of our composition near the middle or not of the paper matters a great deal. How can we know where the middle of the paper is except by considering the edges? Then again, the shapes of paper shut in between the outer parts of the pattern and the edges of the paper or the frame matter a lot to the pattern; they really make a part of it. If such and such a tree, or such and such a book in a Still Life, comes nearly to the edge, whether it comes quite to the edge, or nearly to the edge—and then just how nearly—makes a lot of difference to the balance of the pattern. And good balance is everything. Don't say: 'Oh! but I am not making a picture, I am only making a drawing!' because we have seen already that we must never, in the smallest, most hurried drawing, forget the pattern; it is the pattern which tells us whether we ought even to draw or leave out some part of the subject! So how can we neglect the pattern or anything which influences it? I am really at a loss what to call the things that are done 'all over alike' from a 'copy' or a 'sphere'.

The great painters never did things like that. To call a drawing by Michelangelo and one of those things by the same name is really a kind of blasphemy.

.   .   .   .

Just let us look over once more what I have said about this question of what to draw. I have said: 'Only draw things which interest you'; but then I have added that it is not enough that they should interest you in *any* way. Perhaps the way in which they interest you has very little to do with their appearance, in which case, of course, however much they may interest you, they are not at all suitable for being used as models for drawing from. Then I have told you that this book is about all sorts of things which I am sure you will find very interesting when once I have pointed them out to you—all sorts of things connected with shapes, and light, and shadow, and the ways in which plants and trees grow, and so on. Perhaps in another book I shall tell you how to remark, and study, and understand what that beautiful thing colour is and means. But for the present I think we shall do better only to trouble about drawing, because that already means taking notice of a very great number of facts. At any rate, I hope that when you have read this book once or twice, you will find many more things of interest than you did before you began to read it.

We had already, in the very first pages, seen that there may be quite a lot of good in scribbling, so we tried to find out what is the difference between good and bad scribbling. In order to do this I showed you how to 'take to pieces' a 'composition' by Claude, and I pointed out to you that 'composition' is only another word for pattern. Then we saw at once that the difference between good and bad scribbling is that the good scribbling makes a pattern, while the bad scribbling does not. So we see at once that you are a long way on the road to knowing how to draw, when you know something about pattern-making; because, however you scribble, the pattern doesn't matter very much, so long as the pattern itself is a good one. However badly you scribble, if your pattern is a good one the result is good; some of the best etchings are hardly more than scribbles when we come down to it : only the scribbling makes a good pattern. I want you to give up entirely the idea that there is anything to learn about how to do tricks with a pencil or a pen, or ways of making your drawing 'like'. We now understand that any kind of a line in its right place in the pattern is a good line, while the same line in its wrong place is a bad line. The goodness or badness has next to nothing to do with the line itself; all depends on where it is put in the pattern. So you had better learn as much as you can about picture pattern-making, and only try to draw things which you see beforehand will make good patterns.

III

WHAT TO DRAW WITH

I SUPPOSE you won't be happy if I don't tell you something about what tools you should use. I would rather not say anything about it, so anyhow this chapter will be a very short one ; I am only writing it in order to please you, and you really mustn't expect me to be too amiable —artists very seldom are.

Most amateurs believe that there is great virtue in splendid outfits for drawing and painting, and the makers of these splendid outfits encourage the amateurs to buy these outfits for a great deal of money. The colour-merchants also insist on your buying expensive drawing-papers, which must be thick enough for you to rub out a great many lines a great many times. They also want to sell india-rubber. Now I am going to tell you a secret. A lady friend of mine, who is a very interesting artist indeed, does most of her drawings on ordinary blue-squared arithmetic copy-book paper ; the blue squares which show through the drawing are quite fun, they help the pattern a lot. I myself do all my own drawings from the living model either on ordinary foolscap writing-paper or on some white or whity-brown thin wrapping-paper. I am afraid that Whatman's and other estimable makers of drawing-papers would soon have to shut up shop if they only depended on the trade I bring them. The scribbles I am making for this book I am making on the same paper as that on which I am writing. The way in

which I like drawing from the model is to pin or clip thirty
or forty sheets of thin wrapping-paper to a portfolio (or
a drawing-board) in front of me by the top corners only.
When a drawing goes wrong, I don't worry much about
correcting, and I never rub out; I just throw the sheet
over the back of the drawing-board, and start in on a new
drawing without loss of time. You will learn a lot more by
doing a dozen quick drawings at one sitting than ever you
will by taking a lot of trouble over one only. I have already
told you why : because each time you try to put things
in their right places is a new bit of practice, a new step
towards getting them right straight off. You are learning
to draw things ; you are not learning to correct drawings.

I don't like pens myself, for reasons which I have
explained in some of my other books. One of the reasons
for which I would much rather you did not use a pen is
that a pen is very apt to make you draw 'with your fingers'
and with your hand resting on the paper. DON'T do that.
Always draw with your hand quite free ; don't even 'draw
with your wrist'; draw from the elbow and the shoulder
with the wrist quite stiff. That is the best way to avoid the
nasty little niggling way of doing things that is too often
seen. Also don't lean over a table to draw; draw on
a nearly upright board in front of you, and either sit or
stand at some distance from it. Draw as nearly at arm's
length as is convenient. This will give a free certainty to
your work which you will get in no other way. Set your
board or portfolio up on one chair, and sit on another if
you like. Most children draw naturally with a fine free
line when they get hold of a bit of charcoal or a bit of

chalk, and draw portraits of their friends on a wall, but then if they get into the hands of a bad drawing-master all liberty goes at once out of their work ; they are made to lean over a drawing-board and submit to slavery. Slavery and art have nothing in common.

You can do lots of things, after all, with a pencil and a piece of paper. If you are going to make a shaded drawing you might as well use some kind of specially black pencil, such as a Hardtmuth 'Negro', or a Wolff, or a Conté, because dark shades put in with a black-lead pencil get shiny and disagreeable. If you use charcoal you will have to use with it a slightly rough paper ; any wrapping-paper will do—you need not buy 'Michelet' or 'Ingres'.

Drawing in charcoal is quite different from drawing with a pointed instrument like a pen or a pencil ; so rubbing out in some ways of using charcoal is not real rubbing out, it is not correction ; it is part of the way of drawing, just as putting on the lighter parts of an oil painting is part of the way of painting. We can 'draw' the high lights in a charcoal drawing with a piece of bread well kneaded, or a piece of the modern kinds of india-rubber specially made for this purpose, a soft india-rubber that one can knead into any shape.

But I rather think I should like you to use a brush and Indian ink, at any rate sometimes. Don't get little brushes ; always work with fair-sized ones. One brush as thick— the hair part, I mean—as a good-sized pencil is *all* that you want, provided it comes to a good point when you wet it. You should try this in the shop before buying the brush. It needn't be an expensive sable : I like a good camel-hair brush better. I myself use Chinese brushes of different hairs, often rabbit. A flat oil brush is often very useful in painting in water-colour, in spite of what the shopman may tell you. Indian ink you can either buy in a bottle or as a stick which you must rub down in a saucer as you want it. Don't bother about buying paper strained on cardboard, it is not worth while yet: you have a lot to learn before you ought to try to make the finished drawings for which it may be necessary. At first you will find a lot of difficulty in judging the amount of water to take up in your brush. Beginners never use enough water in wash-drawing; always make a rule of using as much as ever you can, you will soon learn to keep it from running all over the place. You can make a water-colour drawing on an upright board after a little practice. When you have done a lot of work, you will *feel* somehow or other just how much water you ought to take. Sometimes I stop just before putting my brush on the paper, because I *feel* I have too much or too little water in my brush. How I feel it I am sure I don't know; it is the result of habit. Lots of things in drawing are the result of habit; that is why you should make as *many* drawings as you possibly can and not waste time over correcting. *You should learn the 'habit' of MAKING drawings, not the habit of correcting them.* Of course, a nice tidy drawing that has been rubbed out hundreds of times during the term and then finally touched up by the drawing-master may be very nice to take home and show to people who don't know anything about it, who don't know how to paint real pictures themselves; but it doesn't take in people who really know, and you will have learnt next to nothing by doing it. How many young ladies 'do' beautiful prize drawings at school and have them framed, and then are not able to make the slightest sketch once they have no longer got their draw-ing-master behind them, or when they are asked to do something else than a 'shaded drawing from the sphere' in three months!

Well, I told you that this chapter would be very short. I don't think I want to tell you anything more about the ways of making drawings, because there is only one way of making good drawings, and that is to make a lot of them, and above all to study Nature very carefully indeed. When you have learnt to see properly and intelligently, it really doesn't matter on what and with what you put your observations and ideas down. The important thing, the only thing, is to have observations and ideas to put down, so go ahead and practise observing and making ideas of patterns and ways of using a pencil or a brush just as hard as you can. And make hundreds and hundreds of drawings on any old bits of paper, as many as you can, ONLY never make a drawing without observing the model carefully and thinking about what you are doing. Your first drawings will be very weak and bad, but as you go on they will get better and better, till one day they may get very good indeed. Never draw things 'out of your head'. Never draw houses and steam-engines and motor-cars as you think they are; you will be doing yourself harm. You should never make a single stroke on the paper without having first looked at the model before you. If you draw out of your head you are making a drawing without studying, and you will be making a bad drawing. The only way to make a good drawing is to study the model; the goodness of the drawing is the number of things that you have observed on the model, it is not the way in which the drawing is done. If you have no model you can't have any 'goodness' in your drawing.

.   .   .   .

As I have recommended you to use a brush and Indian ink sometimes, I shall add a few hints about managing water-colour washes, which very often won't stay where they are put. I have already told you to use, as a rule, as much water as you possibly can. Most beginners smudge on nearly dry colour, which at once looks dirty. There are times, when we are quite sure of what we are doing, when it may be useful to drag on some dry colour in order to produce a difference in the 'technique', in the way of painting; but to begin with we had better leave that way of doing things quite alone. When you have quite filled a nice big brush with liquid colour put it on the paper without any hesitation. *You should always make up your mind beforehand exactly what you are going to do, and not begin to do it before you are quite sure of what you are going to do.* Never 'try that, to see if it looks all right'; never begin to do something without knowing how you mean to finish it. If you are not sure of what you are about, your work will be weak and worthless; all the great masters were quite sure of what they were doing. Quite a lot of the quality of their work lies in this. Look how sure Claude was of how he was going to put down this pen line or that brush-mark. No great man bothers about correcting and rubbing out, or if he does correct, he always leaves the first line in its slightly wrong place. That's what you must learn to do too. Have the courage to leave your mistakes visible; don't be dishonest and hide them by rubbing them out. That means that what you are interested in is making a tidy drawing instead of being, as they were and as you ought to be, interested in studying Nature. The more you know about Nature the less mistakes you will make in your drawings, and the better they will get.

Be quite sure, then, what you are going to do with your brush; if you mean to cover a large space of paper with a wash, begin at the top of the space and lead the colour down slowly. If you have used a lot of water, the wash will run down to the bottom of the space; rinse your brush in your glass of water—always have plenty of water—dry it quickly on a rag, and take up the extra colour with the dry brush. If your wash is not dark enough, go over it again *when it is quite dry*, then the colour underneath will not come off the paper and mix with the new colour. When you put on a second wash be very careful not to go over the same place twice with the brush, otherwise you will stir up the first wash—now wetted again—and make a mess. It is as well to wet the paper beforehand with clean water and let it nearly dry—I mean let it be only a little damp, not wet. This will prevent your first washes from drying too quickly, before you have done leading them about. Don't bother about 'washing out' any more than you bother about rubbing out with india-rubber. Make a new drawing instead.

IV

SHAPES OF THINGS

WHEN people look at things they get mixed up with a lot of *unimportant* little shapes. It takes quite a lot of study to see at a glance which is the most *important*, the principal, shape of a thing. The French artist Cézanne, who has had such a lot of influence on modern painting, told us that the shapes of all objects can be understood to be only a very little different from the simple shapes that we learn about in our elementary geometry, and that we meet with all the time. Such shapes are : the ball or sphere ; the solid that is called by a long name in geometry, but which we can call 'box-shaped'; the cone ; and so on. I forgot perhaps the most important : the cylinder like a garden roller or a broom-handle. Now any tree trunk is of course very nearly like a cylinder in shape, yet lots of people when they sit down to draw a tree trunk make it look quite flat ! I want you to pay all the attention you possibly can to making your tree trunks look round. Yes, but the paper is flat ; if we make lines on the paper how can we make these lines make the paper look round ? or, to say the same thing in other words, how can we make one part of the paper seem to be nearer to us than another ? Part of the way to make one part of the paper look nearer to us than the other is called *Perspective*. People didn't always understand perspective ; for example, the ancient Egyptians knew little or nothing about it. In Europe it was mostly invented in the fifteenth century, not so very very long ago. I am not going to worry you with a lot of explanations about this rather difficult affair, but I must just tell you one or two things about it.

If you look down a long straight street, you will see that the two sides of the street seem to come together a good long way away from you. The street doesn't seem to be anything like as wide as it is where you are standing. If you are going to draw the street you must imitate this look of it in your drawing. Also you will notice that although the street may be quite level, the far end of the street seems to be a little higher up than it is where you are standing. If you can, go upstairs in some house and look down a street from an upstairs window; you will notice that the end of the street seems to be very much higher up than it seemed to be when you were on the ground. If the street were long enough, you would be surprised to see that the end of it now seems to be as high up as the upstairs window you are looking out of. If you are making a drawing of the street from the window, you must make the lines of the pavement slope right up your paper just as they seem to do in nature; you must make them slope up and slope together at the same time.

When you look out over the sea, or over a great big level plain, the far-off line that seems to be the end of the sea or of the plain is called the horizon. If you are standing on the beach, that line seems only to be as high up as your eyes. If you climb up to the top of the cliffs, if there are any, you will notice that the horizon seems to climb

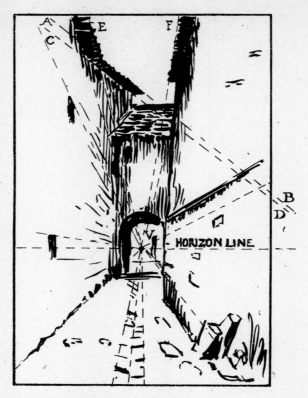

Fig. 18 is a diagram done from a sketch made at La Cavallerie, a curious old village in the Causses in the south of France. The diagram is not quite the same as the sketch which is reproduced in Figure 35; I wanted to draw your attention to some perspective facts. The real street was so crooked and all over the place that I should not have been able to explain what I mean if I had not straightened it out a little. When things are like this you should straighten them out in your mind a bit before putting their crookedness down. This will keep your crookedness in good order. Notice that the street seems to go up the paper till the sides of it would meet at a point straight in front of you and on the Horizon Line which is at the height of your eyes. Parallel lines, such as AB and CD, the edges of the overhanging tiles, finish by meeting at a point on the horizon line. The other roof lines, E and F, meet at V because they are parallel and go straight away from us.

up too; it still seems to be at the height of your eyes, which are now ever so much higher up than they were before. *The horizon always is at the height of your eyes.*

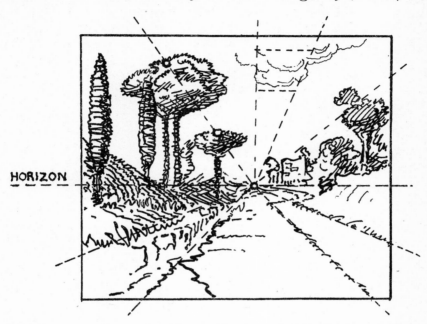

FIG. 19 is a diagram done from a sketch on the Via Appia near Rome, in Italy. It is meant to show that although there may not be any quite straight lines, such as the edges of a pavement, or the top of a wall, or the roof of a house, you must not think you can do without remembering your perspective. You must imagine lines drawn along the tops of trees of about equal height, you must fancy lines running under the clouds, and place your clouds, if they seem to be at the same height from the ground, upon an imaginary table seen in perspective.

It is very important to decide just how high up on your picture the Horizon Line comes. It is important for the following reason: We often come across lines which are parallel to one another, that is, which are always at the same distance from one another. The two sides of a street are an example of parallel lines; the sides of a river are generally about parallel. Now if any set of parallel lines goes either directly away from you, or somewhat sideways away from you, although in reality these lines are parallel they will appear to run towards one another. Just look along any street and you will see that what I say is so. The importance of knowing how high up on your paper the Horizon Line comes is that *all such parallel lines seem to meet, if prolonged, exactly at a point on the Horizon Line.* This is so whether they be up in the air, like the edges of roofs, or down on the ground like kerbstones. Before you begin to make a drawing, first decide, *on the subject,* just where the height of your eyes comes on the model, on the tree trunk, or on the house, or even in the view of the field that you mean to draw; or, in other more learned words: *Make up your mind just where 'the Horizon Line cuts the subject'.* Because: *All the sets of parallel lines* (except those which are 'parallel to the Picture Plane', that is, which cross what we are looking at exactly from right to left without going away from us or coming towards us at all), *whether above or below the Horizon Line, meet on it.* Those which are above slope downwards to it; those which are below slope upwards to it.

I think that you will be able to understand all these things much better from looking at Nature and from looking at the illustrations which I have drawn for you, than if I spend a long time talking about them in words. And after all—if you do as I keep on telling you to do: study Nature, study the model or subject before you, and put down what you really see instead of whatever you think you might see—you ought to have no need to understand perspective at all, even to make quite good drawings. If you are drawing the street you have only to notice very carefully just *how* the lines of the two pavements seem to come together, and just *how* high up they seem to meet, or would meet if the street were long enough; if you put those 'just hows' down on the paper your drawing will be all right. But if you try to make a drawing half out of your head, if you don't look very carefully at what you are drawing; if you don't take the trouble to notice '*just how much*' such and such a gutter of a roof seems to slope downwards as it goes away from you; if you don't notice *just how much* the edges of the book lying on the table seem to slope together and upwards away from you;—if you pay more attention to your drawing than to studying all these things on the model, then your drawing is sure to be all wrong.

. . . .

It is mainly because we see the edges of things slope in the different ways I have been describing that when we look at them we understand that they are solid. If we imitate these slopes in our drawing properly, we shall be inclined by habit to think that the things drawn on the paper really are solid instead of only being flat paper. That, then, is one of the ways in which painters make us think that, in a picture, things are really solid and are placed one behind the other. Another way I have already told you about on p. 4; it is because we are used to seeing one side of a thing darker than the other. If we both make the edges of the thing in the drawing slope right, and worry about the shadows as well, it will begin to look quite solid and very like the thing itself. If we do all quite properly, it will almost be impossible to believe that the thing we have drawn is not really solid, and has not a real shape that we could take hold of.

But just now I have spoken about making things look as if they were one behind another. Next time you go out for a walk, stop in front of some open space that stretches away as far as possible. Look at the things which are near you, or rather choose something near you, and then choose something at some considerable distance away from you, and then again choose something a very long way away indeed—some miles, if possible. If you can, choose the same kind of thing in each case : say a tree. The first thing to notice is that the tree nearest to you is much bigger than the one farther off, and the one farther off is bigger than the one farthest off. This ought not to surprise us, because we have already seen the houses get smaller and smaller and the street get narrower and narrower as it went away from us. Suppose that in front of each house in the street a tree was planted, and that each tree was the same height as all the others, it is quite easy to see that the trees will seem to get smaller just as fast, and no faster, than the houses. We can quite easily imagine that if all the houses were knocked down, that would not alter the appearance of the trees at all. So that if, in a plain, we have a lot of trees in front of us, they will seem to get smaller and smaller by the ordinary ' rules of perspective' just as houses or books which have straight edges. If we have a row of trees of about the same height we can imagine a straight line lying along their tops, and it is not difficult to understand that this line will seem to slope down towards the 'Horizon Line' if we are standing on the same level ground from which the trees grow.

So much for the size that the trees seem to be, but that is not all I want you to remark. I want you to notice that you can see all sorts of things—markings on the trunk, separate leaves, and so on—on the first tree, but on the second you see much less, and probably on the third nothing at all. So in your drawing you must put a lot more 'detail'—that is what we call all sorts of small shapes which are included in the big shapes of our picture—into the first tree than into the second, and probably none at all into the third. Still this is not yet all that I want you to remark. The tree nearest to you is perhaps a dark green. Carefully compare this colour with the green of the second tree, which we will suppose to be about the same in reality as that of the first tree. You will find that the green of the second tree seems much lighter and greyer than that of the first tree. When you come to compare the colour of the tree a long way off with that of the second and with that of the first, you will perhaps find that the tree a long way off does not seem to be green at all, but only a light bluish-grey (of course for this you must choose a tree far enough off, perhaps a mile or two away). This lightening and greying of colour is due to the air (especially when it is damp and slightly foggy) between us and what we are looking at. The more air there is the less we see the colours of objects and the lighter they seem to be. *This lightening and greying on account of distance is called Aerial Perspective.* When we are making a drawing we must pay attention to it and make things lighter and simpler as they get farther off. I hardly ever see children pay any attention to this. They draw and paint things half a mile off in their pictures as darkly and as strongly coloured as those which are in the foreground (or front) of their picture. I hope you will take great notice of aerial perspective.

.   .   .   .

Oh yes! I know that I am taking a very long time in talking about all sorts of things instead of setting you to work at once with a pencil and a piece of paper to learn to draw. That's all on account of the stupid idea that I have got that learning to draw is learning to see, is learning what the real shapes of things are and just how those shapes appear to us. Of course it is a very stupid idea; the only thing that consoles me at all is that Leonardo da Vinci made just the same silly mistake. Well, I still go on thinking that, if you take a pencil and try to draw things without having looked at them very carefully first, and without having noticed all the things I am telling you to notice, you will make a very bad drawing. And I don't see the good of making bad drawings if we can avoid it. Now take, for example, this question of aerial perspective that we have just been talking about. Is it going to help you to study the difference in colour and the differences of lightness and darkness between the three trees, to have a pencil and paper with you? If you begin to make a drawing you will pay attention to a lot of other things and you won't pay as much attention as you ought to the one question of studying these differences of lightness or darkness—'*difference of value*' we artists call it. One thing at a time is quite enough if we do it really properly, and I have no better advice to give you than to recommend you to get into the habit of comparing as often as possible the lightness or darkness of different things, to '*compare their values*'. One of the weakest sides of the English school of painting is just that the values are very rarely treated properly. It is not so easy as you may think to decide whether a white house with the sun on it is lighter or darker than the sky. Try next time you have the chance. Hold your thumb up in front of the house, and then in front of the sky, and see if it gives you the same feeling in each case, or if it looks darker against the sky than it did against the house, or the contrary. Try to decide, in the same way, whether the grass with the sunlight on it just in front of you is lighter or darker than the blue of the distant hills. It is often very difficult to decide, yet, if you want to make a good drawing or a good painting, nothing is more important than this. The Impressionists went so far as to say: 'Drawing is values!' In everything except in pure outline work you must always be asking yourself the question: 'Is this lighter or darker than that?' If it is lighter or darker—and it almost always is—then ask: 'By *just how much* is it lighter or darker?' All this kind of study can be done without ever making a mark on paper; and until you are pretty good at such comparisons it is not much use your trying to draw. Making the observation correctly is all the difficulty; putting the result down on the paper is nothing. It is very difficult to make people believe this, but it is so.

.   .   .   .

So with regard to the question of making shapes look solid; we have three ways of doing so, all of which three ways we can use at the same time if we like. We have: (1) Shadow and light; (2) Linear Perspective—that is the perspective of lines, the lines that we saw running together as they went away from us; and (3) Aerial Perspective, or the lightening of the tints as they are farther off (of course you must understand that a very dark object some way off will always be darker than a very light object quite close up, but it won't be *so much* darker than the other, as it would be if they were both at the same distance from us). It is all this sort of thing that you should be studying and thinking about all the time. Notice for example just how a motor-car driving away from you fast seems to get lighter and lighter in colour—compared with a tree close to you— as it gets farther and farther away.

With all these three ways of doing it we surely ought to be able to get our drawings to 'look solid'! When we sit down to draw something we must first ask ourselves just where the Horizon Line is; this will give us a hint as to how all our lines are going to slope (we can have a good look at whatever parallel lines there may be, and see that they really do seem to slope towards the Horizon Line). Secondly, we must make up our minds as to exactly where the light is coming from; this will tell us how the shadows fall if there are cast shadows (we can have a good look

again and see that they all are on the opposite side to
the light). Thirdly, we can set about comparing the
'Values' (the lightness and darkness of the colours) in
the foreground (the front of the picture) with those in
the 'middle distance' (a little farther off) and with those
in the distance, if we are drawing a landscape. In any
case, whatever we are drawing, we must take a great deal
of care to compare *all* the values, *all over the picture*, with
one another *all* the time we are drawing. When I paint
a picture I *never* leave off comparing the lightness and
darkness of everything in the subject with the lightness
and darkness of everything else in the subject. Then, after
you have done all this thinking and made up your mind
about all these points, you can begin to draw.

.   .   .   .

A little way back I said that Cézanne had told us that
all objects could be looked on as being more or less like
the simple geometrical solids. Each time you have to draw
anything, remember this, and however careful you are to
study and draw the 'detail' of the thing, or the pattern on
it, *never forget its main shape for a moment ; never forget to
keep this main shape 'solid'; never forget to keep it in right perspective*; never forget that all *the pattern on it, all the details
on it, ARE ON IT, ON its surface*. You must never draw
any bit of detail, so to speak, for its own sake, and forgetting that part of what the detail has to do is to lie on
the surface and even to *suggest* the surface by the way in
which it is drawn. If you draw leaves on a tree you must
not draw them in such a way as to flatten the tree out, as

is so often done ; the leaves must be made to look as though they 'lay round' the main shape of the tree. If you draw the cracks in the bark of a tree trunk you must make the cracks look as though they 'lay round' the cylindrical shape of the trunk. If you draw the pattern on a cushion the pattern must 'lie round' the swelling form of the cushion. So even if the pattern is—shall we say?—a simple circle, you must not think you can go ahead and draw it without looking at the model, because that simple circle will be twisted all out of shape 'over' the curved surface of the cushion in such a way that you really won't be able to imagine it. It is just study of all these things that gives a feeling of rightness to your drawing.

It is here that lies the great difficulty of drawing. In drawing we have to pay attention to so many things at the same time. We have to pay attention to : (1) Com-position, because we have already seen that the same line in one part of a drawing or in another may be right or wrong accordingly, may be a necessary part of the pattern or a meaningless scribble. It is the pattern or composi-tion which even tells us if we ought to draw something or leave it out altogether. In the Claude drawing (Fig. 11) Claude has drawn some leaves at C (right-hand bottom corner), but although there were pretty certainly other leaves on the left of the picture, he hasn't drawn them because the pattern didn't want them there. To have put in 'detail' there would have 'dragged the eye down' into that corner, instead of letting it climb up by the fisher-man's net to the tree group and so on into all the rest of the picture in the distance.

Then : (2) We have to pay attention to which side the light is coming from, and put in our shadows also accordingly. Again : (3) We must not do anything without making up our minds just how light or how dark it is to be, compared with all the other things in the picture. We must study our 'values', as the artists say. Once more : (5) We mustn't draw in anything without remembering all about our Horizon Line, and our perspective slopings together, and get them about right. After that : (6) We must be sure not to lose sight of our big simple shapes—look in the Claude (Fig. 11) how carefully the solid egg-shape of the upper part of the trees is kept evident in spite of all the smaller modelling of the leafy branches. Each branch exists by itself, is solid, well thought out ; its shadow sides and light parts are studied, *and yet* it fits into the whole egg-shape quite properly ! That is what is very difficult to do ; very few artists succeed in doing it well ; this is one of the chief reasons why Claude was a great painter. When we try to do that sort of thing we find ourselves either obliged to leave out the detail in order to keep the main shape, or while we are paying attention to the detail, to the smaller branches and leaves and things, we forget the whole shape and forget to fit the leaves and so on into it properly. This sort of thing is not understood by people in general any more than it is by inferior artists. When people see a nice lot of detail, a nice lot of leaves, a nice tidy drawing or painting, they are quite content ; they never ask themselves if the main shapes have been respected, have been reproduced, have been *drawn* properly. Such people say : ' I don't see why you make such a lot of fuss about Claude ;

his drawings aren't half so nice as So-and-so's; they aren't even finished'! Nine times out of ten when you see a very highly finished picture with lots of detail—lots of leaves, lots of blades of grass, and so on—you may be pretty sure (unless the picture be by an early Italian painter, or by some one similar) that the artist has put in the detail because he can't do without it. When it is in, it so bewilders the person who is looking at the picture that he fails to see what the picture *hasn't* got, that is, correctness in values, and properly understood main masses. That explains why people who don't know anything about painting get taken in by pictures that aren't worth anything at all. Such pictures are manufactured by the dozen, and very little is paid to the artist (?), who paints them in next to no time, because he hasn't got to think at all. He just rubs some dark colour on the canvas, and then dots it over with lighter leaves almost anyhow and finishes quite a big picture in a day. Then the dealer gives him 30s. for it, and puts it in his shop window marked thirty guineas. That is how the public is taken in by the picture-dealers, and the understanding of art is lowered. I don't want you to be taken in in that way. That is why I am taking a lot of trouble to explain to you what drawing ought to be, what it is when great artists practise it, and what, alas! it so often is not when practised by most people, even when they are members of all sorts of royal societies who hold annual exhibitions in the West End of London. You may never be able to be a great draughtsman yourself, for great draughtsmen are born with that gift, but I don't see any reason why you should not learn to know good drawing from bad, and not only learn to know good drawing when you see it, but to take a great delight in it, and in art in general, perhaps a greater delight even than those who practise art themselves, and who often, while they understand more about a picture by another artist than any one who is not a painter himself, are still obliged to reserve their enthusiasm for use in their own work, and for Nature who inspires them.

.   .   .   .

Perhaps now it will be time to go on and to give you some examples of just how you should look at things, of what you should specially notice in them, of how you *might* put those things down on paper. I say *might*, for although the same things should be noticed by all artists when they look at Nature, still no two artists put them down on paper in the same way. One artist exaggerates this fact and leaves that one out, another does just the opposite, but all great artists deal with the same facts however they may treat them. It is these facts that you must learn as well as you can to distinguish.

I have decided to use trees for the greater part of my examples; I think you will see why on reading the book. If I talked about the artificial forms of pots and so on, I should not be able to call your attention to the shapes which result from the way in which things *grow*, which is very important. If I had my way I should send you all to the life class. Nothing else is equal to the human figure for practice if you really want to draw.

Some Explanations of Diagram Figure 20.

In the first place we notice that the Horizon Line is just a little lower than half-way up the picture; this is quite a good and usual height to take for it; though, of course, no one obliges you to do so always. You remember that the Horizon Line is just at the height of your eye. If you sit down, the Horizon Line comes lower down at once. In this diagram it is supposed that the artist is standing up, but on ground two or three steps lower down than the flag-stones on which the columns are standing. So if some one of the same height were standing beside the lowest bit of column, he would just about be able to put his elbow on the top of it. Because, of course, you understand that his eyes would be above what is the Horizon Line for the artist, so the artist's Horizon Line must cut across the other person somewhere *below* his eyes. This allows you to find out just how tall a figure ought to appear in the distance; if the figure is that of a person of the same height as yourself, and that person is standing on the same level ground, then your Horizon Line must pass through his eyes. If the ground on which he is standing is higher or lower than that on which you are standing, then you must place his eyes just so much higher or lower. If you are sitting down to draw, then the eyes of grown-up persons will all be above the Horizon Line if they are standing on the same level as that on which you are sitting. And so on. You can always find by this method what the height of a person would be on the same level at a certain distance; and then place that

same height higher up or lower down at the same distance ;
because a person standing on the top of a flight of steps
will, of course, seem to be of the same height as if he or
she were standing at the bottom of the steps, but at the
same distance off.

FIG. 20 is a perspective diagram of which full explanation is given in the
text.

Then we should notice that as the top of the smallest
bit of column comes at A, just at the same height as the
horizon, even though the column is round, we only see
the edge of the top as a straight line. At B the top of that
column is a long way above our eyes, so we see it quite
round, or, more exactly, half-oval in shape. At C the
bottom edge is below our eyes, so we see it half-oval

again ; but this time the oval is curved the other way up. In the diagram of the chestnut tree (Fig. 23) you will see that I have paid attention to this rule ; you must always remember it too.

But before telling you this I ought to have told you that there is a point called the *Point of Sight*, marked V in the diagram. All the lines that go straight away from you, like the pavements of a street down which you are looking, or the gutters of the house roofs along the sides of the street, or the edges of the flag-stones in the diagram, or the edges of the block of masonry—all these lines, which are really parallel, are really the same distance apart— appear, when you look at them, to meet at this one point V, the Principal Vanishing Point, which is always not only exactly on the Horizon Line but *exactly opposite your eye*. It is always as well *not* to put this Vanishing Point (so called because all the lines in question seem to 'vanish' there) exactly in the middle of the picture. It is very nearly in the middle of this diagram, which is one of the many reasons why the diagram is not at all interesting as a picture. I put it nearly in the middle in order to be able to draw my perspective lines with less chance of confusion.

The column which is lying on the pavement does not go straight away from you, so that although its sides are parallel to one another (that is, it is the same width all along), its sides do not 'vanish' to V. But, as all parallel lines (except those straight *across* the picture) must, its sides vanish on the Horizon Line. Lines which are at exactly half a right angle (45°) to the Picture Plane,

that is, lines which are just half-way between going straight
away from you and going straight *across* the picture like
the edge of the step in the diagram, such lines 'vanish' in
two special points called *Distance Points*. The two Distance
Points are just the same distance on each side of the
Point of Sight; and, what is more, this distance from the
Point of Sight to either of the Distance Points is exactly
equal to the distance from your eye to the Picture Plane.
But there, perhaps you don't quite understand what I
mean. What I mean is this: Suppose that the picture
were a sheet of glass, through which you were looking at
a real landscape. You could, of course, trace with a brush
dipped in ink a drawing of the landscape just as you see
it *if you keep your eye quite still in one place.* If you don't
keep it still, you will get in a terrible muddle with your
lines, which will seem to move about over the sheet of
glass as you move your eye. Now the distance of the
Distance Point from the Point of Sight is the same as
the distance from your eye to the pane of glass. I should
recommend you either to draw on the window-pane, if
you are allowed to, or to get hold of a bit of glass and fix
it up in front of you, and draw on it.[1] That is perhaps the
very best way to get to understand this rather difficult
subject of perspective. Because it is much better not to
worry at all about all these geometrical lines, but to simply
learn to 'feel' how to make a thing look solid, look
'round' if it ought to, or square if it ought to. If you carefully notice the appearance of things through a piece of
glass, as I have just told you to, and thoughtfully mark

[1] See p. 149 for description of the method.

a few of the main lines with a brush and a little thick ink, in a very little time you will find that you begin to know quite a lot about how perspective lines go, and you need not worry about vanishing points and distance points and so on at all. With a very little practice you will 'make' things 'look' right if you take a little pains to study their appearances thoughtfully.

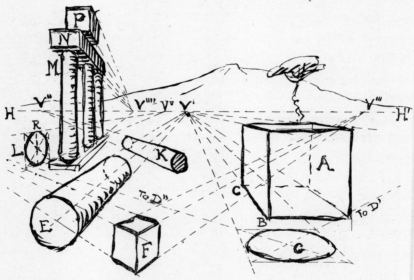

Fig. 21 is another perspective diagram to call closer attention to the shapes that cubes, circles, and cylinders take on when seen in perspective.

You should notice that the way in which you should draw a circle in perspective, a wheel, or a hoop lying on the ground, or the round basin of a fountain, or the edge of a tea-cup or saucer standing on the table, is to imagine it surrounded by a square. Then you 'put this square into perspective', as in G or in L (Fig. 21), and draw the oval that the circle becomes in a free-hand way in the square, but so that it touches all four sides and looks 'right'. While you are drawing it you should keep on feeling that it is *really* lying on the ground, or *really* standing up more or less 'sideways on' to you. That is better than any amount of 'geometrical construction'. Try to think that the real circle is there *in* (not *on*) the paper, and that all you have to do is to follow its shape with the pencil. It is no good *trying* to make it look right, putting it like this or like that to see if it comes right. You must really *see* the real circle *in* your paper and just run the pencil round it. It is useful to notice that the farther half of the oval, which a circle becomes in perspective, is smaller than the nearer half. Thus in L the point R is a little farther away than half-way across the square. So if you are drawing a round arch seen in that way the top of it seems pushed over a little away from you. V^{II}, V^{III}, V^{IIII}, V^{V} are all different Vanishing Points because the different objects to which they belong are more or less askew. V^{I} (Point of Sight) is the Vanishing Point of the things which are square on, and of which the side lines go straight away from you. All the Vanishing Points are on the Horizon Line, all the same. The Columns 'vanish' to V^{IIII}. The square and its circle L 'vanish' to V^{V} to the right of V^{IIII}. So if L were the wheel of a cart going into the picture, and if it kept on in the same direction, it would soon run into the columns. One very often sees carriages, drawn in a street scene, which seem to be being driven all askew, and to be running into the pavement. That is because the artist has not taken care to use the same Vanishing

Point for the wheels of the carriage as he has done for the street pavements.   Just the very most hurried little bit of 'construction', just drawing lightly in, or even imagining, one or two lines to the Vanishing Point on the Horizon Line, will save you from making this very disagreeable mistake.   You see that even my badly and carelessly drawn circle at L looks right and you see just where it would run into the columns.   If I had drawn it to the Vanishing Point V^{IIII} it would have looked as though it were running safely along the side of the columns.

The square round the circle G is quite 'square on' to us.   So the sides vanish to V^{I}.   Now the diagonals of that square are just 'half-square on' to us.   If we 'produce' them, if we carry them on, they will meet the Horizon Line in D^{I} and D^{II}, which are the two Distance Points (see p. 73).   In this diagram they are both outside the picture, and are at equal distances (they always are) from the Principal Vanishing Point V^{I}.   I don't think it is really necessary to worry you any more about this ugly diagram.

V

CONCERNING A CHESTNUT TREE

IF I were able to talk to you really I should like to take you up to objects and explain their main shapes to you, and then show you how I should use those shapes myself in a drawing. As I can't do that I shall have to content myself with reproducing photographs from Nature and point out on the photographs what I want you to notice specially. Now I DON'T want you to copy either the photographs or my diagrams from them. I have already told you that it is very little use copying from 'copies', because they are already flat. By so doing you are learning nothing about 'seeing solid'; you are not getting into the habit of understanding what you see when you look at a *real object*. This is by far the most difficult part of the training of an artist; you must practise it as often as ever you can. Don't copy my diagrams, because they are only diagrams and not drawings. In order to make quite sure that you see what I mean, I am obliged to exaggerate. If I want to point out to you that you must not forget a certain squareness somewhere, I have to make my diagram just as square as I can, but I only want you to *remember* that there is a certain squareness there, not to *make* your drawing really square. If you remember that kind of thing, that is all that is wanted. *When you really think about a thing your drawing will always show that you have thought about it.* That is, again, why a drawing by a great master is so admirable, because we see everywhere in it how he has thought about everything, even about the things he has left out. People who don't understand drawing don't see that he has thought about these things, because, not knowing about the things themselves, they do not recognize the fact that they have been thought about. If you study this book carefully, and study Nature at the same time, you too will be able to take this pleasure in drawings by Michelangelo, by Rembrandt, by Puvis de Chavannes, by Wou Tao-tseu (Godoshi).

What you must really do is to make a drawing from which it would be possible to make one of my diagrams, but which is not evidently like one of my diagrams. When I tell you about the shapes of a chestnut tree, go out of doors and find a chestnut tree and study it, and then draw it for yourself FROM THE SOLID TREE IT-SELF, remembering all I have told you about it, and looking at the tree itself to find out whether I am right or not.

I happen to have some nice photographs of trees taken in that beautiful island in the Mediterranean, Corsica. I can hardly do better than use them because art treats of beauty. Every time you draw you should choose beautiful things to draw as far as you can; that is why I do not wish you to draw all sorts of ugly white-painted cylinders and spheres and things in a dismal classroom. Art is the religion of life and beauty; it is wicked to set unhappy students down in front of dead and dismal ugliness in order to learn art. I choose to talk to you about the beautiful landscape of an island in the Mediterranean.

FIG. 22. This is a photograph of a chestnut tree in Corsica. The subject has been very well chosen by Monsieur Arlaud, who took the photograph. I need not repeat what I say about it in the text.

Just now I spoke about a chestnut tree. I happen to have a photograph of a very fine old chestnut tree in Corsica. We have quite a lot of things to learn from this photograph (Fig. 22).

A tree trunk in general is cylindrical in shape, but some-times, as here, it seems to have left its original shape a good long way behind ; though perhaps not quite so far in reality as might appear if we were looking at a bad draw-ing done from it by some inexperienced draughtsman.

The first thing I do is to decide at what height the Horizon Line comes. If I were really drawing on the spot, the height of my eyes would give it to me ; I should only have to hold a pencil a little way in front of them, and horizontally, to see about where it would cut the tree trunk and the rest of the landscape. But here we have only the photograph to guide us. How are we going to find out where the Horizon Line comes ? I notice that, at the top of the church campanile or bell-tower, the pro-jecting part just below the little dome makes one straight line, although one part of it runs along one side of the tower and the other along the other side. Now, our experiment in the street should have taught us that if a horizontal line is above our heads it seems to slope down-wards as it goes away from us, or if it is underneath us it seems to slope upwards. Now, the line along the side of the tower, which is about face on to us, of course remains horizontal ; but why is the line that goes away from us horizontal too, as it evidently is, because it is in exact prolongation of the other ? If this line which goes away from us is exactly horizontal it neither slopes up nor down, it is neither below nor above our eyes; that is to say, it is at just the same height as our eyes, or, in other words, the horizon runs across the picture at exactly that height. That is how I fixed the height of the horizon in this particular picture. If the sea horizon had been visible, as it might have been quite easily, that would have settled the matter at once. While we are talking about this, just notice that the two lines, one on each side of the road (one of them is a stone wall and the other a row of stones along the edge of the road), meet, if they are prolonged, on the Horizon Line just about where it cuts the tree trunk. You can easily see this by laying two rulers along them. What does this placing of the Horizon Line mean? It means that we are looking down on everything which is below it in the landscape, and that we are looking up at everything which is above it; so we shall see part of the tops of all the solid shapes which are below the Horizon Line, and part of the under portions of all the solid shapes which are above the Horizon Line. Always remember this; it is a great help in keeping your drawing from being flat in appearance; it makes it look real.

Now let us look at the diagram of the cylindrical shapes that I have made of the chestnut tree (Fig. 23), and refer to the diagram (Fig. 20) of the different views of cylinders. We can apply these views at once to our branches. If you will take the trouble to study my diagram a little and compare it with the photograph, I don't think there will be much need for me to explain it any more. You see that I have carefully noticed that the branch A comes a little towards us, and that the branch B, on the contrary, goes

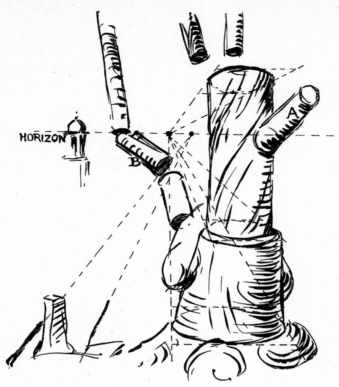

HORIZON

FIG. 23. This funny-looking diagram is to show you how you should always feel the geometrical shapes underneath the irregular ones. Also how these cylinders must be 'put into perspective' just as those in Figures 20 and 21. I have marked two of the Vanishing Points in this diagram: one which belongs to the lines of the road; the other belongs to the tree-trunk circles and is the Principal Vanishing Point. The road does not run quite straight into the picture; that is why it has a Vanishing Point of its own, quite close to the main one, though. You see how I have used the squares in order to get the trunk circles into perspective. Of course I don't mean you to do all this when you draw; I only want you to think about it, and not do anything in your drawing which will disagree too much with it.

M

away from us. *Never draw a branch of a tree, or for the matter of that anything, without being quite sure whether it comes towards you or goes away from you, and, if it does one or the other, by exactly how much.* It is very tempting to go on drawing branches without bothering about this, but if you do your drawing will be bad. Better draw in only two or three branches properly thought out, and leave out all the rest, than draw in dozens carelessly. However *tidily* you draw them in, if you haven't paid attention to the way in which they come towards you or go away from you, your drawing will be weak and worthless. However hurriedly you scribble them in *after* having noted these facts, your drawing will be good. Look at the Claude drawing (Fig. 11) again and see how *very exactly* he has indicated the precise direction towards us and away from us of every branch he has drawn. I have behind me at this moment a big picture by one of his followers in the seventeenth century. It is not so good as a Claude. What do I find on looking at it ? I find that nine times out of ten— and much more often—I cannot tell whether a branch leans into or out of the picture. Almost all the branches are painted flat on the canvas. Yet this is a finished picture and the Claude reproduced in these pages is only a hurried sketch. The difference between a really great painter and only a moderately good one !

.   .   .   .

Let us go on to something else. My diagram of cylinders is perhaps very nice, but after all it doesn't look very much like a tree. What is the matter with it ? It hasn't got anything living about it ; it 's just geometry and

not natural life. Cézanne told us that trees could be compared with cylinders, and he thought it very important to
do so, and to keep on remembering that they were so, but
he did not tell us that trees *were* cylinders. And they
aren't, this one especially! Trees grow, and every kind of
tree has its own way of growing, and this way of growing
changes the cylindrical shape, towards which every tree
tends, into something slightly different. Here is new
matter for us artists. The way of growth of a chestnut is
a spiral or corkscrew way, and this shows in the lines of
the bark. All our cylinders seem to be more or less
twisted. Well, of course we must note this fact in our
drawing. Then this same growth of the tree fits all the
shapes one into the other; the different cylinders of the
branches seem to come out of one another, to 'grow' out
of one another, as in fact they have done. This brings
about a rhythmic joining up of the shapes, which seems to
make the whole tree into a piece of music (you remember
what I said about that on p. 38). If you don't manage to
get hold of that musical feeling in your drawing it will not
be a good one. Each kind of tree has its own particular
kind of music, and one might almost say that each particular tree is a tune by itself. Look how different the music
of the pine tree (Fig. 32) is from that of the chestnut we are
examining now. The pattern of a piece of music, the
music of a pattern, how little difference there really is
between them! And the aim of both is to be beautiful.
Don't make a drawing in order to make a drawing; make
it in order to make a beautiful thing, and in order to admire
attentively the beauty of Nature which you study, from

which you take your inspiration. Drawing is a statement
of beauty; it is not copying things, as so many people seem
to think. Beauty is of many kinds, so drawings are of
many kinds. That is why you hear beautiful drawings
condemned so often by people who have no sense of
beauty, and who say that the drawings are 'not like
Nature', or not finished, or not something. One thing is
certain, that if a drawing is beautiful it is not like the way
in which such people see Nature. If it were it would not
be beautiful. An artist is a man who is gifted with the
power of seeing the beautiful moment of Nature and fully
understanding what makes up that beauty.

.   .   .   .   .

There is one kind of beauty which can be obtained by
putting one geometrical shape beside another. Of this
kind is the beauty created by great architects. Ictinos and
Pheidias, who built the Parthenon at Athens, created
beauty by arranging great simple blocks of stone together.
There was the rectangle of the building, there were the
rows of columns, there were the triangles of the pediments.
All these shapes arranged together in harmonious propor-
tions created beauty. But the beauty was not a living
beauty. To make up for the lack of life Pheidias—and other
sculptors—placed friezes and metopes representing men
and women and horses and centaurs round the building;
and in the triangular pediments at each end Pheidias placed
some of the most wonderful sculpture that has ever
been made by man. You can see it, almost all, in the
British Museum to-day. These bas-reliefs, these sculptured
figures, brought to the whole design a suppleness, a flexi-

FIG. 24. THE ACROPOLIS, ATHENS

The Parthenon is seen nearly in the centre of the picture

bility, a livingness, that the straight, or uniformly curved, surfaces of the building did not possess without them.

When we have understood the arrangement of the cylinders that make up our chestnut tree, we have understood the architectural part of its beauty, but we have not understood the living and supple part of it. And Nature is still more clever than either Ictinos or Pheidias at finding an exact 'balance' (see how often I use the word 'balance'; art is continually a problem in 'balance') between the 'stable', the well 'set down', the well 'built up', the 'architectural', and the supple, the changing, the flexible feeling which belongs to life and to living things. Nature is still more clever than Ictinos and Pheidias because it was from observing her ways that they learnt what they knew about art and about architecture. Nature will always know more about it than we do; we can always go to Nature and learn from her. That is what we are doing now; that is why we have noticed the spiral or corkscrew movement of the lines of the bark, which seem to 'screw' upwards out of the earth towards the sky, just as the tree has grown. They are a motionless record of the upward growth of the tree. If we get this strained upward feeling of aspiration into our drawing, we shall have written down all the story of the growth of the tree ; we shall say without any doubt, 'This thing that I have drawn is a living thing; it has grown, it is growing!'

Then at all the angles of the branches, where they come out of the main trunk and elsewhere, we must notice first how all the angles are rounded off, and secondly just *how* they are rounded off, and how one cylindrical form joins up with another. If the angles were not rounded off, especially on the inside, the branches would be too easily broken off by the wind, or by their own weight. Every engineer will tell you that it is necessary to round off this kind of junction ; by so doing you render it very, very much stronger. There is no harm at all in knowing a little elementary mechanics if you mean to draw. I should advise you to study the subject. Unless you understand how things are made, how they resist strains of all sorts, how they resist the action of gravity, you are not likely to draw them very successfully. Mechanics is the science which teaches you all about that sort of thing. Don't think that because you know about science your art will be spoilt; that is a very mistaken idea. To be an artist you cannot know too much, though you should not always be anxious to show off what you know. You must invent each time a kind of 'balance' between what should be put in and what should be left out. Leonardo da Vinci was very interested in the science of his time, such as it was ; and as we go on, science becomes more and more mixed up with everyday life, and the artist of the future will have to deal more and more with science and her ways.

The great difficulty in drawing is to strike a just balance between (*a*) the 'architectural' structure of things—that is, the placing of the cylinders in this case of a tree ; and (*b*) the flexible, supple structure of living forms. Draughtsmen as a rule exaggerate one or other of these two qualities— unless—as is too often the case—they possess neither! In one sense the two qualities are enemies one to the other; the architectural quality is sturdy and rigid, the

other is yielding and supple. Much of the personal character of a draughtsman is revealed by whether he chooses to
put more of one or of the other into his work. Nature
herself always gives us the most exquisite balance between
the two.

.   .   .   .

You may have heard, or you may hear, a great deal of
talk about 'planes' in drawing. I have not yet used this
word in these pages. Several artists have said : 'Natural
form is never round, it always "turns" by planes.' There
is of course some truth in this. Look at the second tree
trunk in our photograph, the tree under the campanile
of the church. You can see the light side and the dark
side quite clearly separated one from the other by an
almost sharp line. The trunk on this side seems to be
faced with two clearly marked flat surfaces, or *planes*.
Then we have already split up the big trunk into cylinders
with rounded surfaces ; that is all very well for a first big
splitting up, but when we come to look into the matter
more closely, we see that these rounded surfaces can be
split up into facets like those of a crystal. For example,
it is almost one flat rectangular surface (A, Fig. 25) which
runs up from the base of the tree, and is almost continued
in the branch which comes towards us (B). In Figure 26
I have drawn diagrammatically another way of 'looking
at' this tree trunk.

If you wish to make a good and valuable drawing of
such a tree trunk, you must manage somehow or other
to include in your drawing all these three different ways
of 'looking at' it, of 'seeing it' (Figs. 23, 25, and 26).

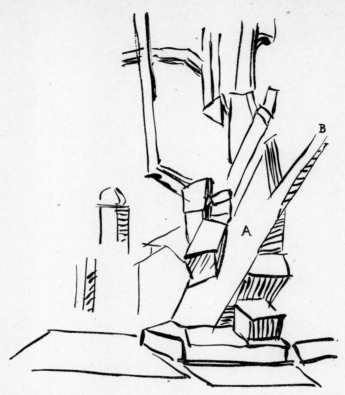

FIG. 25. This is another way of 'looking at' the chestnut tree. This time, instead of trying to see it in round cylinders, we try to see it in flat planes and cubical kinds of shapes. Neither the cylinders nor the 'cubes' are the truth about the matter. Yet the truth of the affair has something of each in it. Some artists make more fuss about the planes, some about the round shapes. That is their business ; I think you will be wise to keep just as well as you can half-way between the two, forgetting neither, but making neither more important than the other. In short, always *think* of both while you are at work, but *do* neither of them. Of course all these planes must obey the rules of perspective, so you should always keep your Horizon Line and Vanishing Points in the back of your head. There are lots of things to think about when we make a drawing. That 's why it 's so difficult to do a good one.

Fɪɢ. 26.   Figures 23 and 25 don't give us all that goes to make up the shape of the chestnut tree.   The cylinders and the cubes and things seem to want joining up, just as the masses in the Claude composition in Figure 14 wanted 'joining up' by the curved lines which are put in in Figure 17.   Here I have exaggerated the curliness of the lines.   The tree, in consequence, looks 'floppy'. Now every one of these three diagrams has been exaggerated ; you must steer in and out among them and make a drawing which is at the same time like all three and like none of them.   It must be properly stood down and built up like the geometrical ones, and yet be living and flexible and just a little bit curly like the third.

You will not find it easy to make an exact balance between all these three different qualities of natural form. Of the three, the solid geometrical way of looking at things seems to be the one which people have the greatest difficulty in attaining: so I should recommend you to practise that most, to think about it most, to exaggerate it most. You can always soften things off afterwards in your later work when once you have learnt how to see the *architectural construction* which underlies the suppleness of Nature. The next most difficult thing to see is the 'planes', though in one sense there is really not much need to make any difference between this and the first way of looking at things. Very often the first way of looking at things will lead you to draw, not a cylinder, but some kind of a prism with flat sides which are the planes in question. The flexibility and suppleness would seem to be the quality the most easily seen, though real masters of it are, after all, perhaps just as rare as those of 'architectural construction'. The general faults of bad drawing, and naturally those which we should try our best to avoid, are : (*a*) Forms which are not properly and rhythmically (musically) joined together, which don't seem to 'belong' to one another, either by their simple placing or by 'rhythmic suppleness'. (*b*) Though they are not joined up, still they do not show a proper understanding of the 'constructional placing of masses' (as Fig. 23); they are disconnected without reason. (*c*) The masses are not properly 'set down' on the ground or elsewhere; they seem to have no 'substance', no 'being'; they seem to float weakly and indefinitely. This is, of course, really the same fault as (*b*), only I wish to call special attention to it, as it is the great fault which is committed unceasingly throughout all the 'nice water-colours' that one sees. People are so surprised when one refuses to admire them, and, I am afraid, put one's want of admiration down to one's disagreeable character! Yet a picture which has not such qualities (I am here talking of a picture which pretends to reproduce the appearance of Nature) has no more to do with art than it has with blind-man's-buff. And though it may come in for a lot of ignorant admiration for a short time during the life of the painter, yet in time to come people will somehow forget it altogether instead of going on talking about it as they do about the pictures of Claude, of Leonardo, of Rembrandt, of all the great masters who possessed the quality of architectural stability in their work. Lastly, (*d*) a want of nervous life and tension in the lines and forms of the drawing. Almost all natural shapes seem to suggest something springing and full of vivacity, even if they are not actually in movement. Take the stem of a flower, or a blade of grass; it may bend over because it is top-heavy, but even then it bends over in a springy way. It is much better to get this springy feeling into your drawing than it is to copy the curve of the stem, perhaps more accurately, but in a dead, lifeless way. One of the main evils of india-rubber and accuracy is that they both kill the life of a drawing; they tend to replace life by tidiness, and tidiness is only one little bit of life, a very little bit of life indeed. Let life loose properly in a tropical jungle and just see if it is very tidy. Tidiness has wonderfully little to do with art. While you are drawing a line you should be quite excited about it; you should wind yourself up to feeling that you are the same thing as the line and possessed of its sentiment. Japanese painters tell us that when we want to paint the gleam of light in a tiger's eye we should feel for the moment just as fierce as the tiger. The sentiment which you feel will come out at the tip of your brush, the Chinese say. If you don't feel anything, it won't come out at the point of your brush or your pencil. For that reason making a good drawing is a very tiring thing; one is in such a state of excitement all the time one is doing it. Most ordinary drawings do not make us feel that the artist (?) was at all excited while he was doing them. That is why they leave us unmoved, why we pass them by, why they are forgotten. The drawings which we remember are those which are architecturally stable ; which show a well - combined pattern (light and shade and all that sort of thing is included in this); and which hand on to us the excitement, the emotion of the artist.

.   .   .   .

As this chapter is about the photograph of the chestnut tree (Fig. 22), I will not leave off writing until I have called your attention to a few other things which we may study with advantage from this picture.

First, you should notice that it is of the type of 'lop-sided' composition. Although it is a ' view' of the church tower and the beginning of the village, an artist looks on the subject as being in reality the tree trunk. For him the rest is 'middle distance' and 'distance'. Yet what you

look at is much less the tree trunk than the road, the
church, and the houses. In the very first place a picture
must be a pattern, but this does not prevent you from
representing interesting things. A very great number of
Turner's sketches are 'views' of towns, but if you take
the trouble to look at them you will find that he never
forgot the foreground. Provided you put them in the
right place and manage your pattern properly, things in
the foreground never prevent you from seeing things
farther off. The great mistake that most inexperienced
sketchers make is that when they want to make a sketch of
some building or 'view' they sit down straight in front of
it, and try to make of it *all* their picture. The experienced
artist does not do like this at all. He is rather inclined not
to worry about his building or his town. That's all right;
he knows where it is, and can find it whenever he wants
it! What bothers him is *to find a suitable foreground*, that
is, one which will work up into a good pattern (always the
base of all painting). A view all by itself hardly ever
makes a good pattern on the paper; all the shapes in it
are too small as a rule, and the lighting is too even; there
are no marked contrasts of light and dark; for lots of
reasons like these a view alone never makes a good
picture. Then when you look at a view, you have things
near you; perhaps a person beside you, perhaps a tree
trunk, as in the present case, which enables you to compare the size of the things in the distance with known
sizes near you. So if you see that a church tower seems
quite small, when it is compared with a person, you know
that it must be a good way off. Now distance, or being

a 'good way off', is quite a necessary part of drawing
a view. As we don't often have set-out perspective lines to
deal with—as we have in a street—we can only depend on
'aerial perspective' (see pp. 61–62) to make it plain that
the things are a long way off. We can make them lighter
and greyer in colour or value . . . lighter and greyer than
what? Why the foreground, what else? But if we have
no foreground we can't make the distance [1] lighter than
it is; so we must have some kind of a foreground if we
want to draw a view successfully. After all, art is little
else than comparisons between things, relations between
things. In a view, the 'distance' is farther off than the
foreground; a view is a comparison between the nearness
of the foreground and the farness of the distance. The
foreground is just as important, and more so, than the
distance in a view. Look what a lot of foreground there
is in this photograph (of course in artistic language the
tree as well, and not only the ground, is 'foreground');
there is quite as much foreground as there is view, and
the thing which attracts most attention, the church bell-
tower or campanile, is one of the smallest of the lot, only
it is just at the 'centre of interest of the composition', at
the place in the pattern which all the facts and masses
and lines of the composition lead us to look at ; so we see
it more easily than anything else. *Now* you understand
another use of the pattern of a picture; it allows us to call
attention to something without making it big, so we are
able to make it small by comparison with big things in the
foreground, and yet, by means of the pattern, so to say,

[1] Or, of course, middle distance.

keep the big things out of the way so that they don't prevent us from seeing the little thing farther off. In the Claude (Fig. 11) we see the bridge quite easily, although it is just sketched in with a few strokes of the pen and is next to hidden by the group of trees, because the lines E and F (Fig. 17) of the composition lead us to it. So the pattern allows us to institute comparisons of size, without which we should find it very difficult to give the effect of distance. You see how very, very important it is to think about your pattern first of all. In practice, when I want to make a drawing of a mountain or a village or something like that, the first thing I do is not to get out into the open, but to look as hard as I can for something to hide behind, generally a tree; in the present case Monsieur Arlaud, who took this photograph, 'hid behind' the chestnut tree, though his real reason for taking the picture was the village and the distant snow-covered peaks. The old and gnarled chestnut tree gave him an admirable beginning of a pattern and brought into the picture all sorts of small things (twigs, plants, and so on) on a big scale in the foreground, with which one can compare the big things on a small scale in the distance, and so get an 'effect' of distance into his picture. Don't forget this use of 'pattern' or composition.

VI

A DRAWING OF A CHESTNUT TREE

I SUPPOSE you won't be satisfied unless I make a sketch of this chestnut tree to show you how I should do it myself. I am very unhappy about doing one, for two or three reasons. First, I don't want to pretend for a moment that I know how to do it at all well myself, because I don't. Then I am fearfully afraid that you may take it into your head to copy my drawing, and you know that I don't want you to copy any drawings, but always to work from Nature herself, and to find out for yourself how immense is her store-house of beautiful rhythms, of splendid patterns, which may be used for making works of art. Then you will slowly learn how to choose those rhythms, those 'musical' harmonies, those patterns *in order of importance*, for yourself. By working from Nature you will be less tempted to 'see flat', always the great difficulty to strive against. But I am not telling you to do things which I don't do myself. I happen to have those photographs of Corsican landscapes which are just the thing for me to explain lots of points about drawing from, so I have been tempted to use them. But at the present moment I am not in Corsica (though I am not so very far away from it), and so I can't go to Nature and make a drawing of the chestnut tree from the real tree. Besides, if I could it would all be different now, for I am writing these words in the month of August, so instead of the bare twigs there are certainly masses of leaves on that chestnut tree, from which the photograph was taken five or six months ago. If I make a drawing from the photograph I am doing just what I tell you not to do; and if I do make it, it won't be anything like as good as it would have been if I had made it straight from the tree. That is precisely why I keep on telling you to go straight to Nature, if you want to make good drawings and not bad ones. Drawing isn't imitation; it's getting excited about Nature, about her rhythms, about her patterns. Then how can I see just what facts to ex-aggerate ever so little in order to make the trunk 'look' solid? I can't find them in the photograph. This brings us to another reason why drawing is not copying; I think you will be able to understand it.

When the photographic apparatus 'looks at' the tree and the village and the mountains, it 'looks at' them with one eye—its lens—and without moving. A great part of our understanding that an object is solid comes from the two facts: that most of us have two eyes, and that we don't stay quite still when we look at things. You have most of you seen, at the Royal Academy or elsewhere, architects' perspective drawings of buildings. These draw-ings are always very nicely done, and the perspective is always quite correct, yet somehow or other they don't seem to be real buildings, there is always something thin and papery about them. There are, of course, plenty of reasons for this, but one of the chief reasons is that the perspective is *too* right; it supposes that we look at things with only one eye, and that we keep that one eye quite still. This is what you never really do, so the proper perspective drawing always makes you feel a little uncomfortable ; you feel somehow that you don't really see things in that way. 'But', you may reply, 'a photograph, this one of the chestnut tree, looks real enough. If it were coloured I should think that I see things just like that.' Well, I have no doubt you do think so, still in reality you don't see like that. I have often tried to use photographs to work seriously from, and I always have had to give it up. The photograph looks more right than the architect's drawing because there is any amount of detail in it ; the shapes, the flattened shapes of things are quite faithfully reproduced; *but their solid forms are not.* Most times you can *guess* at the shape of something on account of the shading, but when you actually get to work at making a good solid drawing from a photograph you find you cannot ; you examine the photograph as closely as you can, but you quite fail very often to get a thoroughly clear idea of the real solid shapes. Perhaps it might be possible to draw well from photographs in a stereoscope, that is, from double photographs taken with two lenses ; I have never tried.

As a result of illness and overwork I recently lost the sight of my left eye. This has quite prevented me from doing the drawings that I used to do. When I look at the model I am not sure just how near or just how far off a part of the surface is ; I hesitate, I am never quite sure, and indecision means bad work. So true is it that we use both eyes in order to see the solidity of things (that is how far different parts of them are away from us), that now I have to be very careful about taking up a glass, or pouring water into it. If I do not go to work very slowly the

chances are that I shall knock the glass over, or pour the
water on the table ; that is, I shall see it as either too near
or too far from me. Some people recommend you to paint
with only one eye open ; they are quite wrong ; their work
—as so much painting is—is certainly thin and flat. Many
illustrators work nowadays from photographs. They are
able to do this because their work is flat. That is one of
the reasons why they are only illustrators, and not great

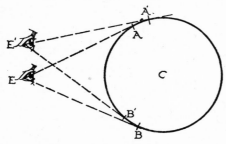 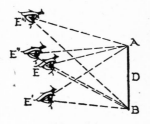

FIG. 27 shows one of the ways in which
you find out or guess that a thing has
thickness when you look at it. I have explained how this is in the text.

FIG. 28 shows two ways
of guessing that a thing hasn't
any thickness. This is also
explained in the text.

artists, such as for example Daumier, who earned a poor
living by drawing lithographic illustrations, but who was
as well a great painter, unrecognized during his life, but
quite recognized now. You can see some of his drawings
in the South Kensington Museum. His work is wonderfully solid.

Why we 'see solid' with two eyes is shown in Figure 27.
Suppose we are looking with our two eyes E and E' at a
cylinder C—I have cut it through in the diagram, so it
only becomes a circle. With the eye E we see as far round
as the point A on one side and on the other side a little

farther round to the point B. On the other hand, with the eye E′ we see as far as A′ on one side, and only as far as B′ on the other. Now when we are very small indeed, only a few months old, we don't yet understand what this means; we don't understand that seeing a thing in that way means that A′ is farther off than A nor that B is farther off than B′; in other words, we don't know how to judge distance at all. Watch a little baby; all the time it stretches out its hand to take hold of something which pleases it on the other side of the road! It is by stretching its hand out like that thousands of times that it begins slowly to learn that, when an object has such an appearance, it is certainly just so far away. Even when we are quite grown up it is only possible to judge the farness of objects fairly close up to us. Even from a few miles off we don't know at all what distance there may be between them. And as for the stars, which are really millions of miles apart, they all look to us to be at the same distance, because the nearest of them is already so far away that we have left off being able to judge distances before we get to it. Of course this leaving off being able to judge distances is due to the narrowing of the visual angle, but I mustn't explain that here. You will learn all about that in books and classes on physics.

Then to this ' stereoscopic vision ', to this ' solid seeing ' (for stereoscopic comes from two Greek words meaning ' solid ' and ' see '), you must not forget to add an unconscious experiment that you are making all the time : you move your head ever so little to one side or the other when looking at a thing, and so a little ' farther round ', first on the left and then on the right ; so you reason un-consciously thus : 'If I can see farther round on moving my head, the thing must have some thickness.' If it were a thin sheet of paper, as in Figure 28, both eyes, E and E', would only see the same point A and the same point B instead of A and A' and B and B', as in Figure 27. Even if we moved our heads so as to place our eyes at E" and E''' we should still only see A and B. We should thus judge at once that AB hasn't any thickness at all.

All this is very nice and simple, but how on earth are we to make any use of it in drawing ? Unfortunately that is just where I cannot give you any rules. If I could, I should be able to teach you at once quite a lot about how to become a really great artist, for it is hardly any but the great artists who really succeed in giving you the feeling of real solid existence of things ; though of course they have other gifts as well. It is part of the artistic gift to guess without making any mistake, and without knowing even that it is being done, exactly what exaggerations to make in order to give the feeling of solidity. There are many ways in which this is done. You will find that great artists, unlike drawing-masters, generally leave in their drawings several lines from which we may choose. As a matter of fact we don't choose, but these several lines play the part of outlines drawn from slightly different places, just as we look at things from slightly different points of view. Such a drawing really amounts to what we really see from two or three points of view all put down, one over the other, on the same piece of paper. As this is a thing we are doing all the time in reality in our minds we are quite ready to accept it on the paper. But this is not by any means all the story, which I cannot go into here, as it would become much too complicated. All I can say is that you must practise trying to find out what facts specially help you to see a thing solid, and then note them on your paper, even exaggerating them a little. You will never make a drawing seem to be too solid! In the Cézanne drawing (Fig. 30), look at the middle of the front

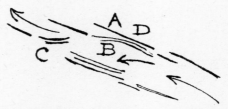

FIG. 29 is an exaggerated diagram of what Cézanne noticed in the middle of the front branch which slopes across Fig. 30 from near the bottom right-hand corner to just beyond the middle of the top of the picture. I have explained this in the text.

diagonal branch and you will see at once one of the things which help us to understand that it is solid. The lines which come up from the trunk for the first two inches do not join up with those which go on above them. I have exaggerated this state of things in a diagram (Fig. 29). Then also you will notice that, as well as the space between A and B, there is no outline at all at C. Instead of an outline there are two or three light, curved lines just a little higher up into the branch ; these, taken with the curved lines at D, make us feel that the branch comes ever so little towards us just here. You would have thought that this was a very

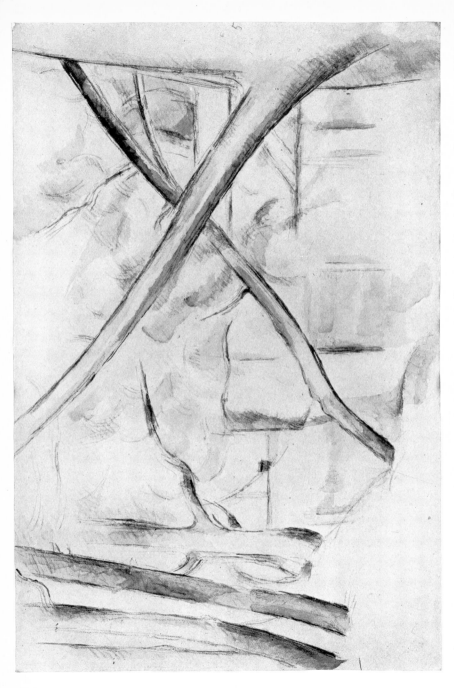

Fig. 30. This is a reproduction taken from *The Way to Sketch*. It is from a drawing by Cézanne. I want you specially to notice how solid he has made all the trunks and other things in this very slight sketch. He has made them all appear to be so many solid cylinders and solid blocks. When he had done that, and had made a good pattern, he was quite content and left off. He didn't mind a bit whether his drawing was 'finished' or not.

careless drawing, not at all finished, wouldn't you ? In fact you would not have called it a drawing at all ; and perhaps you might have thought that you could do as well and better yourself. Yet this drawing which seems so careless is really full of most delicate observation of this kind ; go over it carefully yourself and notice all the places where very delicate modelling is so marked. Look how all the ' comings towards us ' and ' goings away from us ' are clearly marked on the branch which sticks out over the water from the upright trunk at the water's edge. Also notice how Cézanne has *only* marked the solidity of the masses of foliage.

But even if in the photograph of the chestnut tree we succeed in seeing all these facts of solidity, there is still an excellent reason why a drawing from a photograph can never be really good. The real difference between a good and a bad drawing is a question of the enthusiasm, of the excitement, of the emotion which the artist felt when he was making it, when he was looking at Nature. Now a photograph is a very cold makeshift for the living beauty of Nature ; and although I may be able to get *interested* in a photograph, I really can't get excited about its beauty as I can about the beauty of real tree trunks, and grass and rocks and sunlight, and all the countless things that make Nature so beautiful. What makes a drawing good is that some little of this beauty hangs about the drawing in a mysterious way. When you have drunk in the beauty of Nature, it seems to come out again in some not understandable way from your pencil point or from your brush tip.

One can't really do this drinking in of the beauty of Nature from a bromide photographic print; the print is all very well in its way, but its way isn't wide enough. What I really ought to do is to make a drawing from Nature, then photograph the subject, and then, lastly, make a new drawing from the photograph; then you would be able to see at once how chilly and poor the second drawing would be compared with the first. But this means rather a lot of complication, especially as I can't at all be sure of making a fairly good drawing *to order* like that; indeed I should probably make a very poor one, because instead of being simply excited about the beauty of Nature, I should have it in the back of my head that I must do a good drawing for the book, that it must show all sorts of things that it ought to show, and so on. Such an affair becomes business at once and ceases to be art.

About what I have said concerning getting excited in front of Nature: some clever person may say that some of the greatest pictures have not been painted from Nature at all. I must remind that clever person that in this book I am not talking about how to paint masterpieces, but how to begin to learn to draw well, and with feeling. I should have said: 'that is, with feeling', not 'and with feeling'; for a drawing without feeling cannot be good. A great artist who draws upon the excitement of his inspiration as well as on the results of long study of Nature is not quite in the same position as our beginners.

FIG. 31 is a drawing which I have made from the photograph reproduced in Figure 22. I would much rather not have made it, because for several reasons it is obliged to be a bad one. Still it may give you some hints as to the kind of thing I thought I ought to notice in that particular landscape. Whatever you do, *don't* copy this drawing, only compare it with the photograph, and notice what I have used and what I have left out, and how, for example, I have in the foreground been more inclined to show the way the surface of the ground goes than to draw the tufts of grass on it.

Well, anyway, I have done this drawing (Fig. 31) from the photograph of the chestnut tree. I can only hope you may be satisfied. I'm not. But if you haven't much to learn from my successes, you may at least learn something from my mistakes. Do you see—in the photograph—the shadow of the branch lying across the foot of the trunk? I have not drawn it in the drawing. I had put it in at first, but I took it out again because I found that : first, just as it does in the photograph, it keeps you from seeing the shape of the foot of the trunk ; secondly, that although it fits into the *whole* pattern of the photograph fairly well, it didn't at all fit into the pattern of the drawing, from which so many other things (which help, in the photograph, to 'balance' the shadow) are left out. So having put this shadow in, I took it out again because I found that it both helped to flatten the trunk, and did not fit into the pattern properly. In the same way I had put in the bit of branch which one sees just above the fork on the right of the photograph. In the photograph it does not seem to upset the balance of the pattern, but in the drawing, from which so many things are left out, it upset everything, so it too I took out. You must understand that the balance in the photograph is not at all the same balance as that in the drawing. Several parts of the drawing are merely white paper, while the corresponding parts of the photograph are often quite dark tints. It is quite clear that we cannot balance a white place in the pattern by the same thing which has served in the photograph to balance a dark place. So, although you take the *main* idea of your balance of pattern from Nature, you must pick and choose among the facts of Nature and only use what fits into the pattern which you have made up your mind to make.

In order to make quite clear to you that pattern is the most important part of drawing I am using the word very often. But this may lead you into an error. Pattern is the most important part of drawing because it is only another way of speaking of balance, which in some form or another is the very soul of art. The trouble about the word 'pattern' is this: I am afraid that it will lead you only to think of the flat pattern on the flat surface of the paper. If you do this, it will make your work not worth very much. Remember what I said on p. 23, line 29, about being able to make a plan of what you mean to draw. *There is just as much composition or pattern INTO the paper as there is on its surface.* Or if you prefer it (though it is not exactly the same thing) the 'ground-plan' of the picture should make a good pattern just as well as the actual picture which you draw on the surface of the paper. Here again we must be artists and invent a nice 'balance' between the 'mass composition' (or how the solid bodies are placed in the subject we are drawing from; perhaps we might call it the 'solid pattern' of the picture) and the flat pattern on the surface of the paper. Both these 'patterns' must fit together, must quite belong to one another, if we want our picture to be completely satisfactory. Then, also, do not forget what I said on p. 40, line 13, that there are at least two parts of a pattern on the surface: there is the way in which things are placed about on the paper; and there is also the way in which these things are joined up by forms which wind in and out among them. Here again we must still be artists and judge the 'balance' necessary between the two. Almost always, except in the case of very great men, you will find that a composition, a pattern, is too split up into bits, or is too 'curly'. The great compositions in European art are always based on straight lines; the curve is used moderately to add a graciousness to the too great rigidity of the straight.

I have not wanted to carry the drawing any farther, because I wished to show as far as possible the way in which it was done, and what I have chosen, up to a certain point, as the most important facts, which I think will be fairly clear when Figure 30 is compared with the constructional diagrams (Figs. 23, 25, and 26). You may want to know what 'tools' I used. It is drawn on type-writing paper, with Chinese ink. I have a stick of Chinese writing-ink, which I rub down on a Chinese stone. I used a Hardtmuth 'Negro' No. 3 pencil, and a Chinese writing-brush. In some places I used a small 'hog-tool' (an oil brush). I took out the mistakes with some tempera white, which I prefer to the various 'Chinese whites' and 'process whites', because it is less, or rather not at all, gummy.

But there isn't any real virtue in these things which I have used; if I had not been afraid of getting into trouble with the Oxford University Press, and the block-maker, and all sorts of other business people, I might just as well have made my drawing on a bit of calcareous tertiary rock, picked up outside, with a bit of red bauxite (aluminium ore—hydrated oxide of aluminium, stained with oxide of iron), just as some neolithic artist may have done two thousand five hundred years ago here. I did find some lumps of red ochre in a neolithic cave opposite this window a few years ago. The piece of rock would have been rather heavy to send off by post too. These reasons, much more than artistic ones, made me choose the Chinese ink and the 'Negro' pencil; but if you must know what I used—well, there, I *did* use them. If there's anything important about the drawing at all, it's what I *thought*, not what I employed to make the drawing with.

VII

THE BEAUTY OF THE PINE

CHINESE and Japanese artists are very fond of drawing the wonderfully decorative shapes that pine trees so often take. But it is not only on account of the beautiful shapes of this tree that the refined artists of the Far East choose it so often for their drawings and paintings. When a Chinaman or a Japanese chooses a subject to paint he does not choose it for its beauty alone; for him plants and animals— both real and imaginary, such as the dragon—have meanings, 'symbolical' meanings; that is, they suggest ideas to him. Thus the bamboo is the image of virtue and fidelity, the plum tree in blossom that of purity and sensitiveness, and so on through a long, long list. The dragons that seem so queer to you are to the Chinaman the image of heavenly creative power; that is why they are not natural animals, but entirely creatures of the imagination. On the other hand, a tiger to a Chinaman is not simply a wild animal, but the portrait and 'symbol' of earthly force. The pine tree with its knotted, twisted shapes, so often called on to resist the rigour of a mountain storm, is to the people of the Far East the emblem of vital force, sturdy and tenacious. So the Chinaman tries above everything to enclose this feeling of force in the lines of his drawing, in every stroke of his brush. If the pine tree is covered with snow, he sees in it the picture of youthful vigour and strength in old age.

In our reproduction (Fig. 32) there is no snow on the pine tree itself, there is only a little left among the rocks beyond, for the photograph was taken in the spring-time. Notice how much the photograph loses in charm if you cover the patch of snow on the left with your finger; the curved line of the edge of the foreground 'leads the eye' up to the snow patch, which in this way becomes an aim and reason for the foreground sweep. When we reach the whiteness of the snow we are content. While we are noticing the 'pattern' or composition of this photograph, we might also remark how the tops of the rocks in front of the patch begin another curve which we can trace through the branches of the tree quite out to the extreme right of it, where the last branch tips give just a little hitch upwards before they finish and seem to 'run out' in an upward curve parallel to that of the rocky sky-line underneath.

What is our main pattern or composition here? The curved line of the foreground (that is why the snow patch is so useful; it 'finishes up' one of the main composition sweeps) and the curved sky-line of the rocks are the two main curves which are cut across by the straight and nearly upright trunks of the trees (see Fig. 33). That is what we may call the 'line composition', but you understand that I really ought to have begun by talking about the 'mass' or 'volume' composition, just as I did when we were examining the drawing by Claude (Fig. 11, and pp. 31–33). Here, of course, it is again the middle mass of the trees just as it was

FIG. 32. I wanted to reproduce this photograph because it seemed to me to be rather unusually decorative. Everything seems to ' fit in ' so well into the pattern. Then the pine tree is of quite a different kind from trees like the chestnut, or the oak, or the beech. So I wanted to call your attention both to the things which are the same and to the things which are different. It will be a very good exercise for you to compare Figures 22 and 32 very carefully, to notice as many differences as you can between the ways of growth of the chestnut and of the pine.

Photograph by G. L. Arlaud, Lyon

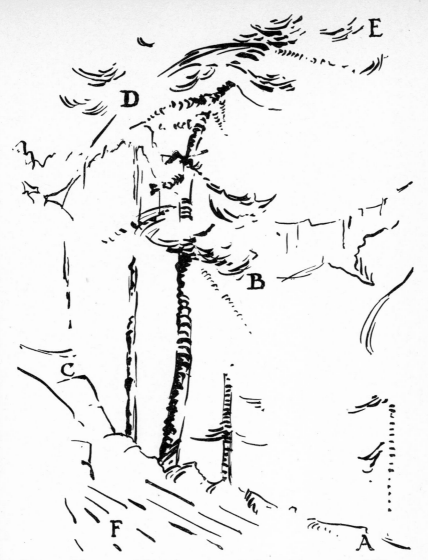

FIG. 33. I have noted down here the main facts of the pattern of Figure 32.
In spite of my best intentions I have made this diagram quite flat, because,
first, I was drawing from a flat photograph, and secondly, I wanted to use
a line-block, and I am in the habit of using differences of 'value' to show
solidity, in a way which would not 'reproduce' in a line-block. Anyhow the
diagram shows the important facts of the flat pattern. We must be content
with that.

in the Claude, but in the Claude the mass of leaves was clear above the ground and 'counted' altogether against the sky. Here all the lower part of the foliage is seen against the grey, against the 'half-tone' (it is half-way between the darkest and the lightest parts of the picture), so does not 'count' as much as the top part of the big front tree. Fortunately it is just this top part which is of the most amusing shape, of the most decorative shape; and that is what really makes such a good subject of this for a picture. Put your hand over the top part of the tree. There is hardly any 'interest' left in the picture. And now remember that the curved line of the foreground 'took' us up to the snow patch, and from there we got quite easily into the curve that runs through the top part of the tree. In any good 'composition' the various parts of the pattern fit in and work together in that way. I don't like the word 'composition' because it makes you think that the masses and lines are 'composed' or made up. This is a photograph from Nature; still you see that we can take the 'composition' to pieces just as we did in the case of the Claude, just as we did in the case of the picture of the chestnut tree and the village. Nature herself more often than not supplies us with most perfect patterns. Some time back I told you to invent your own patterns; I should have done better to tell you to *choose* your own patterns from the natural ones that surround you at every moment. That is the best way to learn how to invent patterns for yourself, patterns which shall be really your own. Look once more how well everything fits in here; the curved line under the mass of foliage and

branches just in the middle of the picture is exactly continued by the dark edge of the trees on the distant crags.
Then the light branch that cuts across the middle of the
curve is just in the right place too. If we shut it out, we
see how useful it is in the general balance. Nature is
wonderfully clever at making up her patterns, even down
to the smallest detail. When you are drawing from Nature
and you find a 'hole' in your pattern, you have only to
look at that place in Nature to find just what is wanted to
fill that 'hole' up properly. The thing you find there is,
somehow or other, just the right shape. Why this is so
we must leave to those very annoying people who write
very useless books on 'aesthetics' to try to find out—
which they won't. 'Aesthetics' is the name given by such
people to a pretended examination of what makes things
beautiful, although in the beginning the word only came
from the Greek verb meaning 'to perceive'. For the time
being we may be content with knowing and feeling that
a thing is beautiful, and noticing that, when it is, it lends
itself to making balanced and harmonious patterns, made
up of all sorts of interworking rhythms.   For the present
we need not trouble more about it.

Perhaps I have forgotten to tell you that what is true of
the big masses and big lines of a 'composition' goes on
being true right down to the very smallest facts and details
of the picture. *Nothing*, not even a little pebble in the
foreground, and close to the edge of the paper where it
will hardly ever be noticed, must be put in anyhow, without
thinking about how it fits into the whole pattern, whether
it is wanted, whether it would be better to leave it out

altogether. It is ever so much more difficult to leave out properly than to put in. The funny thing is that most people leave out all that they ought to put in, and put in a lot of things which really don't matter a little bit. For example, they quite forget to 'put in' the roundness and solidity of a tree trunk, and then get very anxious about crowding as many leaves as ever they can on a tree (?) which never would have the strength to hold them up, seeing that its trunk doesn't seem to have even the thickness of a piece of paper. Hundreds and hundreds of perfectly reasonable people do that kind of thing, seem to take a special delight in doing it. Look at the Claude drawing (Fig. 11) and notice once more how splendidly solid the tree trunks seem, how capable of holding up any amount of leaves and branches. And then how strongly they seem to come out of the ground, and seem to be fixed into it. Paul Cézanne, of modern painters, was the artist who painted this springing out of the ground, this solid, column-like quality of tree trunks better than any one else. Try to get as much of this feeling into your work as you can, and perhaps we shall be spared some of the pretty water-colour sketches with flat, seaweedy trees, which would flop over if they hadn't got the paper to hold them up, and which seem to have no connexion at all with the earth, instead of springing out of it into the air like the jet of a fountain, and spreading afterwards into a tuft of branches so frequently like the drops of water into which the first single jet splits up. Although living shapes are often still, yet they seem to hold shut up in them some likeness to movement. This likeness to movement you must always try your best to draw; it is what will make your drawing alive. 'But how am I to draw movement?' you will ask me. 'And still worse, how am I to draw *likeness* to movement?' I have already told you that what you feel while you are drawing will appear, will come out in your work. Be quite convinced about this 'feeling of movement'; look for it every time you can; get quite excited about it; be quite glad when you find it out, and then with your pencil *mean* to get it into your drawing. If you do all this properly I shall be surprised if a little of it doesn't get hitched into your drawing somehow or other. But if on the other hand you hold your pencil with scrunched-up fingers close down to the point, and rest your hand on the paper, and try to draw by bending your fingers to and fro as you are taught to write with a pen, and if you keep your nose close down on the paper while you are 'trying to draw a tree', and if you keep on rubbing out lines, and paying attention to joining them all up nicely, and making a really nice drawing, I am sure that however 'nice' and 'tidy' and 'black-leady' your draw-ing (?) may be when it is done, it won't have any of these qualities of springing life. The only way to get them is not to bother about the drawing at all, only to get fearfully excited about the beautiful forms of the tree itself. It's the tree that matters; your drawing doesn't matter a little bit. So hold your pencil firmly, and don't move the joints of your fingers, but draw with all your arm, right from the shoulder, and try to put down your feelings freely on the paper, without troubling about putting them down tidily; the 'putting down' will get tidier of its own accord as you

learn to see things properly and quickly and choose the
important facts one after the other *in order*. Drawing is
learning to see, but learning to see—in this sense—is
learning to see in order of *importance*. I am trying to tell
you something about this order of importance in this
book. You must never leave off trying to make out the
real order of importance of things. Very often a little
thinking will do the thing for you. Take this pine tree;
what after all is the most important thing about it from
the point of view of our picture? Surely it is that its trunk
should stand up nice and solidly, and be well fixed in the
ground. If these things were not so, we simply shouldn't
have any tree to draw; it would have fallen down and disappeared long ago. Claude and Cézanne understood this
and 'went for' the solid roundness of the trunk and its
'coming out' of the ground before anything else. A great
number of Cézanne's studies are just tree trunks and
nothing else; just notings of their solidity and springing
out of the ground. He felt that this was so important that
when he had got it down he didn't bother about any of
the rest.

VIII

PATTERN. FINISH. TECHNIQUE

PROBABLY the greatest difficulty that you will encounter, when you begin to draw, will be to notice or to 'see' things which will make good pictures. I have already spoken to you about this in the chapter on 'What to Draw', but feel inclined to say still more about it now, for it is such a very important branch of the subject. If you have chosen your picture, your composition, your pattern, properly, your drawing will almost make itself. The needs of completing the pattern will show you what lines to put in, and what shape they are to take. On the other hand, if you have not got hold of a beautiful pattern you will go on struggling all the time and finish with a very unsatisfactory piece of work. Perseverance of this kind is worse than useless. If you find that your work is not going along easily and well, you had much better stop and ask yourself why it is not getting on. And the first thing you would do well to look to is your pattern. Say to your-self: 'Now is this a *really* good pattern that I am after?' If you have any doubt about it, leave off work, and choose a better pattern, a better composition. If any one says to you that you should show more perseverance, you may reply: 'But I *am* showing perseverance. I am *not* giving up learning to see beauty, which is learning to draw. On the contrary, I am learning to see beauty better by leaving this pattern which I have found out to be ugly, and by trying to find a beautiful one. In this drawing which I am giving up, I have just found out that I have made a mistake in the beginning of it, so it is no good going on with it. If I had said in the first line of a long multiplication sum, "3 times 2 are 7", you would not tell me to go on with the sum in order to show my perseverance, would you? Or a better example still : If I had begun a problem all wrong, say by dividing the number of days that so many workmen took over a piece of work by the number of workmen, instead of multiplying them together, you would not tell me to go on with the problem all the same in order to show my perseverance, would you? You would tell me to start over again on different lines. That is just what I am doing now. I have made the first great mistake in my "operations"; it is no good going on. I had better begin all over again.' In matters of arithmetical problems grown-up people generally know when you have made a mistake in the beginning of your problem, but so very few people, even those who pretend to, know much about that very funny subject, art, that they hardly ever understand what the mistake that you have made is; let alone understanding that it is just as important as that of dividing instead of multiplying in the beginning of an arithmetical problem. They don't understand that no amount of india-rubber and perseverance will make a work of art out of something that is not one from the start ; any more than any amount of multiplication and addition and so on will get a correct result from a problem which is begun wrongly. I will almost go so far as to say that *it is easier to do a good drawing than it is to do a bad one!*

Fig. 34 is a photograph of a bridge. It might be in Scotland, though it really is in Corsica. I have chosen it as an example of a usual kind of landscape pattern or composition, one which you may easily come across yourself.

Photograph by G. L. Arlaud, Lyon

Everything that you do in a good drawing at once suggests what you should do immediately afterwards. Because, after having put in the new line or the new dot, you see at once, as often as not, what must be done somewhere else *now*. Such and such a space did not appear empty *until* we filled such and such another space up. Now it does. So we must fill it up. In turn, when we fill it up, and the drawing looks in consequence more finished, we see that that other part does not look quite finished enough in its turn. And so on. But all these things do not appear unless we keep our balance of pattern going along easily and properly all the time. So *never be tempted to 'finish up' one bit of a drawing before the rest, unless that bit be in a main point of interest,* the most important part of the drawing, the thing which one looks at most. For example, in the chestnut tree (Fig. 22 and Fig. 31) it might be quite allowable to work on the right-hand bottom bole of the trunk and on the top of the church tower, or 'campanile', because these are two important places in the composition. In the bridge (Fig. 34 and Fig. 35) of course much more work can be put in, if you like, at the top of the arch of the bridge than anywhere else in the picture, and if you *must* finish up one of the little trees in the foreground, in the front of the picture, finish up the one nearly in the middle rather than the left-hand one. But, after all, this only comes to the same thing as I have been saying all along: *Only work according to the needs of your pattern.* These needs will keep you quite busy, for as fast as you add a line, or a dot, or a bit of shading, that addition will make a new need felt.

Then there is another kind of mistaken perseverance.

In the National Gallery there are, or there were (perhaps they are in the Tate Gallery now), a very great number of Turner's sketches and drawings. Some 19,000 pieces of

FIG. 35 is a diagram of the chief things which you should pay attention to. This drawing is flat too. Perhaps the real reason why I have made Figs. 33 and 35 so flat is because they are diagrams and not drawings. The way in which one makes things look solid is by observing all sorts of refinements. But if I did this here I should not be able to call attention to the things ; the refinements, which would indicate the things, being refined, you would not notice them. In this case I have only wanted to call your attention to the modelling of the ground, so I have marked its slopes and flatnesses with simple coarse lines. In the solid Cézanne drawing (Fig. 30) all this is done very delicately . . . but then you don't notice it.

paper, I think, generally with drawings on both sides. (This is *not* a mistaken form of perseverance! for they were almost all done from Nature, and with a view to learning about Nature. But, then, Turner was a genius, and knew that he was for ever in need of learning.) Well, lots of these sketches are just two or three lines and a dot or two, all he had the time to put down while the coach or '*diligence*' was driving on. I have always been amazed at the choice he made of just the right *important things of the pattern*. The most rapid of these sketches is a complete pattern, a complete work of art ; *it would be a sin to carry it any farther*, to finish it up any more. It is very rare for ordinary mortals as I am, and as I dare say a lot of you are, to hit off a perfect balance of this kind in just a few lines. If you do succeed, put it aside at once; don't, for heaven's sake, think you ' ought ' to finish it. Take a new piece of paper, if you must go on, and begin all over again. Keep at any price what Browning called so justly. ' The first fine careless rapture '. We don't know how we obtain the finest part of our work ; it is no good thinking that we do. When we produce a really good piece of 'beauty', let us leave it alone. In the case of drawing it never *can* be 'recaptured'. We may, perchance, do something better, but we shall never reproduce the same. How many fairly good things have I spoilt because I thought I ' ought ' to go on with them ! Plenty of things go on all right enough, and come out balanced up after some hundreds of pencil strokes or brush-marks, but the complete sketches of Turner and the monochrome masterpieces of Liang K'ai or of Sesshū are rare flowerings of the human spirit, to be conserved as precious things.

'You must learn to walk before you can run.' No doubt this is as true of art as it is of other things. The trouble is that we must take great care in applying this maxim or rule of conduct. If people tell you : 'You must learn to draw a straight line properly before you do anything else,' they are advising you wrongly. If they say : 'Don't sit down to draw all that view before you can draw a tea-pot and a couple of tea-cups, or the trunk of a tree,' they are giving you good advice, and they are applying the maxim properly. If they say : 'Don't bother about composition yet. Learn to draw before you bother about making pictures,' they are applying it wrongly. If they set you to copy flat copies under the pretence that they are easier to 'do' than drawing from the model, from Nature, you are receiving bad advice. If they tell you you *must* draw with a line, or draw 'by shading', or draw in any fixed way, they are giving you bad advice. It is your business, after you have made a lot of experiments, to decide for yourself what way of drawing you are going to take up. About all these points, except the last, I think I have said enough in the foregoing pages to allow you to understand why I give you these rules. But with regard to the way in which you make the marks on paper, which we call drawing, I might perhaps add a few words.

The underlying necessity of a good drawing is pattern or composition. Now one pattern should not necessarily be carried out in the same way as another. *The kind of pattern we choose should decide the way in which we are going to draw it.* One of the very first things you must do, on deciding to draw something, is to ask yourself *just exactly* what it is that has drawn your attention to the subject— where lies, *exactly*, the charm of the picture? In one case it may be a question of charm of outline, in another an

arrangement of light and shade. Now it is quite plain that
it is no good trying to draw a light and shade subject in
outline, or a 'flat' lighted pattern of an arrangement of
edges in shading. So we see once more how all-important
a careful understanding of pattern or composition is. We
can't even know whether we ought to take up a sharp-
pointed pencil to draw with, or a water-colour brush full
of Chinese ink, until we have quite worried out the question of composition. *The nature of the composition suggests
the way in which we should draw it.*

The kind of composition suggests the way in which we
should draw it. Of course the kind of thing we are drawing
must also be taken into account.   Figure 18 is drawn from
a light and shade wash-drawing (Fig. 36) which I made on
the spot. The shapes are hardly interesting at all. The
overhanging roofs and the rounded archway have some
little picturesqueness in themselves, but if you make a line-
drawing in thin line of such a subject, or even if you make it
in thick lines as I have done in the diagram (Fig. 18), hardly
any of the reason why I made my original sketch subsists.
What made the charm of the subject was the mystery of
light and shadow on the walls of the narrow alley, and the
still deeper shade under the archway. I realized this, so
that was what I drew. It was no good drawing outline
shapes with a view to making a sketch of a thing which only
makes us want to draw it on account of the gentle shading
off of its shadows, or on account of its depth of dark. It is all
very well to make an outline drawing of a thing such as the
Parthenon on the top of the Acropolis (Fig. 24); the columns,
the pediments, the other ruins, the shape of the rock itself

R 2

all make decorative outlines ; we can, if we like, under certain circumstances make a pure outline drawing of such
a subject.   Not always though ; suppose we are looking at
the Acropolis against an evening sky, we shall feel a certain kind of emotion, a certain kind of feeling that it is
beautiful.   I don't think it is any good trying to put aside
that particular feeling which we have, and which is made
up of a feeling for the dark mass of the rock and the
ruins against the light evening sky, in favour of quite
another kind of feeling for pure outline of shapes.   Let's
put down what we feel at the moment ; let's scribble in
the mass of shadow of the rock and ruins and so make a
sketch quite different from the one we might make of the
same subject in the morning ; when, lit from the same side
as that on which we are standing, the rock and buildings
hardly count at all on light and shade for their effect.   You
may think that it is very easy to see why you think that
a thing is beautiful.   I can assure you that sometimes it is
not at all easy ; the greater number of inferior pictures
are inferior because the artist has not known how to put
his finger on exactly the reason of the beauty.   He sees
that there is something to be made out of such a subject ;
but when he gets to work he pays too much attention to
things which don't matter, and nothing like enough attention to the *important* things.   It is the old question of *importance* coming up again.   Sometimes I am inclined to think
that it is just about the whole story of art.

I don't know how to recommend you to learn to recognize
the importance of things, compared one with another ; I am
afraid that the only way is to do a lot of studies.   Sometimes

FIG. 36. SKETCH OF STREET IN LA CAVALLERIE

This is from a sketch made on the spot. It is meant to show how, in this case, the most important thing to note is the grading of the shadows, and not the shapes of things as one can draw them with line. It should be compared with figure 18, from which *all* the interest of the original, here reproduced, has disappeared. The play of light and shade can make bare and uninteresting subjects interesting.

you might make experiments in drawing an outline study, a half-outline half-shadow study, and a full light and shade study of the same subject, and then see which looks best. Or you might go and look carefully at paintings by Rembrandt and compare them with paintings by the early Tuscan masters such as Piero di Cosimo, or Piero della Francesca, or many others of the period before 1500. They all counted on the clearness of their outlines, while Rembrandt lays himself out to do without outlines at all, and to lose all the edges as far as possible in shadow. When you have seen the kind of thing Rembrandt painted in this way, and the kind of thing which the others painted in their way, you will be a good long way towards understanding whether it will be better to use outline or light and shade in order to make a drawing of something which you have seen and which has pleased you. You will understand better *why* it has pleased you.

'Something which has pleased you. I was out for a walk yesterday evening, and coming home I suddenly saw a long beam of evening sunlight cutting diagonally across the road. I have walked up that road hundreds of times and have never noticed the subject of a picture there. Yet had I had my colours with me yesterday I should probably have made a sketch. A sketch of what? That is just the point. *A sketch of the beam of light*; that was what interested me. I should have fitted round it I don't know what trees or rocks or bushes just to fill up. And when it was done you would have thought that I had painted those trees, rocks, and bushes as a subject. That is very often the great difference between an experienced artist and an amateur. Most amateurs and beginners want to paint *things*; they want to paint the gateway of a town, a picturesque old house, a view, without paying any attention to whether it will make a picture, whether it will make a pattern. Now in the ordinary course of events my road didn't make a pattern at all, or at any rate only a poor one. But the line of light with the shadow on each side and the high bank on the right *did* make a good pattern *at that particular moment*, and would have made a much better picture than the picturesque old gateway at the entrance to Les Baux which hundreds of enthusiastic painters keep on trying to paint, and which always, in spite of its Renaissance architecture, stubbornly refuses to make a good picture pattern, because there is too much on one side and not enough on the other, however you arrange the lighting. Wise people would say to themselves : 'Why does that gateway please me ? Is it on account of the pattern it makes? No. It is because it is old and picturesque, and, *in itself*, well designed. So I will admire it for being old and picturesque and well designed, and I will not make a sketch of it; but I *will* make a note of how that tree shadow runs up the wall and arranges itself over that rock ; because, although under ordinary circumstances there is only a bit of rock and a wall there, *at this moment* there is a wonderfully beautiful pattern of shadow to be drawn.' Several times I have made a sketch of the corner of my room when the western sun throws over the furniture the shapes of the woodwork of the window. At other times the same corner is not interesting at all.

Although it is undoubtedly an addition to a picture that

the things painted should be interesting in themselves, still you must never let yourself draw or paint interesting things so arranged as to make a bad pattern; far better paint uninteresting things well arranged than the most interesting things badly arranged. And you will find that however interesting be the badly arranged things the resulting picture will be uninteresting; while, on the contrary, the uninteresting things well arranged will make a very interesting picture. *Because the picture isn't the things themselves; a picture is an arrangement.*

    .   .   .   .

'Yes,' you will say, 'but here he goes talking about pictures again instead of about drawing!' A drawing is a picture, or ought to be, or *must* be. Any other kinds of marks on paper may be instructions for building a house or for making a machine. As such they may be excellent in their way, just as diagrams of all sorts are; I have made many such 'drawings' myself; but I am not writing about that kind of 'drawing' in this book, I am only writing about drawings which pretend to be classed as works of art. And the two classes of work are just about as far apart as possible. Who would make a 'working drawing' of an evening beam of light lying across the road? Yet that might have been the subject of a drawing or painting which, chance has it, I have not painted. It is true that there the principal attraction was the colour, yet a monochrome drawing of it would not have been worthless either—a drawing in light and shade, of course. On the other hand, the original (Fig. 36) of Figure 18 was made almost in monochrome, as the colour hardly counted at all in the attractiveness of the subject. When you mean to try and make drawings which shall be even modest works of art, it is no use thinking that 'inartistic' exercises will help you at all, that you will in any way learn from them 'to walk before you can run'.   On the contrary, they will probably prevent you from ever 'running' artistically.

.   .   .   .

Figure 37 is the reproduction of a photograph by an amateur photographer. There was a picture, there were many pictures to be made out of the subject, but unfortunately he just succeeded in missing all of them. In Figure 38 I have made a diagram of at least one possible picture. (Always supposing that the bit I have added out of my head at A was like that, or something like that in Nature. If it was different I have but little doubt that it was *better* from a pattern point of view than what I have indicated.) Our photographer did not know how to use the pattern, or rather one of the patterns of which Nature gave him the hint. The dotted lines BF, FA, CG, and so on, will show what I mean at once. In the photograph they are not placed in a balanced way 'into' the paper. I think I see why he placed the whole subject so low in the picture. It was because there was a fine mass of clouds in the sky of which he wanted to get a photograph. That is just the sort of thing we must always have the courage *not* to do. It is an example of photographing the thing on account of its interest as an object, without thinking out properly whether the result is going to be a good pattern. I don't think you can fail to feel that there is something a little wrong with the balance of the

FIG. 37 is the reproduction of a photograph by an amateur photographer. I have reproduced it to show how he has not made a good pattern out of his subject, although there were many to be made. Notice how the picture seems too low in the framing and the upper part empty in spite of the clouds. Compare with Figure 15, where this is not the case.

photograph, and that there is less wrong with the diagram. You may not think that this matters very much, and may imagine that you can go ahead and draw without bothering about such things. The diagram is near enough to being a drawing to serve for the moment's argument; at any rate, you can see what it is meant to be. Let us examine

FIG. 38 is one suggestion (out of many) which I make for improving the pattern of Figure 37.

how it is done. At A there is the supposed line at the top of the trees and the half-dozen brush-strokes just over the letter A. Why have I put in these brush-strokes? For two reasons : (*a*) because they hint at the solid roundness of the mass of trees; (*b*) because *they are at A.* They make the point A at the end of the Horizon Line, and at the end of the imaginary line FA. They make an important point in the composition, *otherwise they would not have been put in at all!* If my pattern had not been properly thought out to begin with, *I should not have known what lines to make at all*; I should have gone on muddling round, putting in things at haphazard; I should have made a weak drawing, or in other words : *Without having a good pattern to go on, I should not have known how to draw.* The man who made the photograph does not know how to draw, so he left that part of the picture out altogether! Knowing how to draw and knowing how to balance up a pattern are one and the same thing. There is nothing at all wonderful about the half-dozen brush-strokes at A; you could make them just as well as I can. If you don't believe it, just for once copy them! What you might not know how to do is to have put them there, because you hadn't worked out the pattern. The same kind of reasoning applies to every one of the other three or four dozen brush-marks that make up this diagrammatic sketch. Amuse yourself by putting little bits of white paper over different lines in the diagram, and note how you wish them back again, because without them the pattern no longer balances. You will in that way see at once why I put them in. 'How clever to do it with so few lines!' one is always hearing. Not at all clever to use only a few lines; the whole secret lies in the choice of the important parts of the pattern. When they are done, the thing can remain like that.

Figure 39 is a cherry tree growing at the top of the bank. I chose it because it seemed to make a good pattern altogether, and because we can see on it nice and clearly the sturdy pushing outwards of the springy form

FIG. 39 is the reproduction of a cherry tree. You can notice the springing form of the branches, and their fan-like arrangement *in all directions*. It would be more exact to call it a cup-like arrangement. The roots form part of the pattern here.

FIG. 40 is a photograph of a palm. It shows another kind of arrangement of the branches. Note how very 'broad' the 'effect' is. Almost all is contained in two values : the sky and path, and the dark. The shadow on the path is a third value with the house. Put the picture a long way away from you and study the simplicity of the patterns in dark and light.

Photograph by G. L. Arlaud, Lyon

of the branches, with their general outward trend like the opened fingers of the hand. You must always get this feeling of radiation into your drawings of trees and plants. Each tree and plant has its own way of radiating. Some radiate sturdily; some in a drooping way, like the weeping willow; some half-way between, like the palm in one of the Corsican photographs (Fig. 40). A good draughtsman will make you feel intensely the character of the radiation, of the fan shape of each tree. As I have said before, sacrifice strict exactitude to free obtaining of this sentiment of the way of growth of a tree or plant. Then again, don't draw the palm branches flat on the paper: notice in this case how the branches turn on themselves. Look how the biggest branch in the photograph starts nearly horizontally and then twists on itself and is set on edge at its outer end. You will notice that as a result the lower leaves are foreshortened, while the upper ones are seen quite sideways on. You should look at the Claude drawings and notice how all these things are carefully noted by him. (There is a drawing of a palm in Gowans's little book.)

To return to our cherry tree; you will notice that I did not set it low down in the paper because the roots give us occasion to make up an interesting pattern. The most interesting parts of this pattern I have traced in the diagram (Fig. 41). One thing to be remarked is how at A there would be an empty space if those two or three little branches didn't happen to be just there. There always are things 'just there' in Nature to help you out with your pattern. All you have to do is to look for them.

Here, you see, the little branches lean towards the trunk of the tree just as they ought to for the pattern. They seem to buttress up the tree, and to lead the eye back to

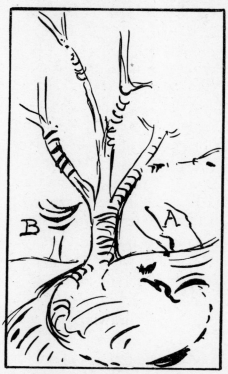

Fɪɢ. 41 is a diagram showing the main facts of patterns which made me choose the subject of the cherry-tree photograph (Fig. 39). (The branches at A appear too important. They were drawn too thickly for a line-block.)

the main point of interest, the place at which the trunk splits up into three. You might think that these branches, being very thin and little, may quite well be left out. That is not so. Of course they *could* be left out; but if we did so the drawing would lose very much more than it

FIG. 42 is a photograph of a group of trees intended to
call your attention to the way in which several trees com-
bine to make a simple arrangement of shapes.   Two other
things are to be noticed : that there is not enough foreground, so the pattern is bad, and the trees do not seem to
be ' held up ', ' supported ' properly ; and that the photograph seems to be quite flat, in this case not only because
of the ' one eye ' of the apparatus (see p. 98), but also on
account of wrong exposure, which puts all the ' values '
out.   The Impressionists said : Drawing *is* values.

would lose if we left out things which are much bigger
and darker. For example, I have left out nearly all the
foliage in the diagram except that at B, which is, after all,
no darker there than elsewhere, or hardly; only in the
pattern it is more *important* there. Once again, the pattern
teaches us what to put in and what to leave out.

.　　　.　　　.　　　.

All the shapes of a tree or plant balance one another in
a remarkable way. But not only do the shapes of a single
tree balance one another, but if you look at a group of
trees you will find that the trees which make it up all fit
into one pattern. Look at Figure 42. There are four or
five big trees there, yet they all fit into the same decorative shape: all the smaller curves of the outside edge fit
into one great big curve which runs right round the group.
In the Claude drawing also (Fig. 11) we see how all the
trees fit together to make one decorative group shape.
In the photograph (Fig. 42) you will notice how very
difficult it is to see the directions to and from you. This
really thick-through group of big trees looks quite flat on
the paper. It would be very difficult to make even a
moderately decent drawing from such a photograph, so
I will not try to at all. This photograph, too, has been
taken much too low down in the paper. To make a good
pattern the top line of the branches should have been
right up at the top of the picture. People rarely make
the mistake of putting too much foreground.

CONCLUSION

DRAWING is a statement of beauty, a putting down on paper or elsewhere, by means of lines, of dots, of smudges, a representation of what makes the things around us look beautiful to us. Whether drawing may be all sorts of other abstruse things as well we will leave to cleverer people to decide. If you want to learn to draw you must learn to delight in beautiful things. 'But what is beauty?' of course you are going to ask me. I am very sorry, but I don't know. I may have ideas of my own as to what it may be, but I don't think I will bother you with them. 'But some people "like" one thing and some "like" another—how am I to know which person is right, when they don't agree?'

Recognizing beauty in all its forms is not by any means as easy as most people think it is. And there has been quite a lot of ugly quarrelling over what is, and what is not, beautiful. For the time being I think the best advice I can give you is this: In the first place study very attentively all the natural forms of plants and trees and rocks and bits of broken stone that you come across. Their forms are always beautiful in some way or another. Then go and study the pictures of the really great artists, Leonardo da Vinci, Turner, Rembrandt, the greatest Chinese artists, Greek sculpture, as much as ever you like. But be very careful not to look at modern illustration; or at the work of some contemporary painter, because every one is talking about him. Mind, I don't mean to say that his work must be bad because he is modern: I have spoken a lot about Cézanne in these pages, and he has only been dead quite a few years. I tell you not to listen to popular opinion on the matter, because popular opinion is generally wrong in these cases, because so very few people really know anything about art. I tell you to go and look at the 'Old Masters' because, there, fashion exists no longer; the people about whom a lot of fuss was made when they were alive are often, now that they are dead, quite forgotten. Even though people in general don't know much about art, still, when generations and generations of artists and critics have decided that Rembrandt 'will do', we can be pretty sure that the verdict is not far wrong. When, like Cézanne, you have learnt to appreciate the 'Old Masters' properly, to understand just *where* the 'beauty' of each picture lies, then you may begin with safety to apply what you know to judging the heaps of modern pictures that you see, and to bring to their judging also all that you have learnt from Nature herself about her ways of beauty. If you have done all this properly, I am afraid you will remain very dissatisfied with most of what is done to-day. Not because it is modern, but simply because it isn't good enough; it is too full of ignorance. When I look at a drawing or a picture, I like to be able to say: 'Well, how did he ever think of doing that like that? I should never have had that idea. If I only knew all that about the form!' In front of most modern work I say: 'Hides what he doesn't know under that clever (?) little trick with the brush. That pen drawing "goes down" because it's so tidily done; people don't see what he doesn't know because they don't know it themselves. There is some kind of a distance between that drawing and one by Michelangelo!' Of course you are young and will delight in the art of to-day, so do I—when there is any good in it—although I am so much older than you are. I was brought up amid the making of modern art, and one of the next books I am going to write will be about the technique of modern art. But I am very frightened about telling you to go and study it too closely at first, because it is too new, and the judgements about it have not yet had time to settle down as have those on Rembrandt and Velasquez. Also because a great deal of it is very bad indeed. It is so very easy to do a drawing quite like that by Cézanne (Fig. 30), and yet quite worthless. It is very difficult to do one which shall contain all the delicate observations, some of which I have pointed out to you. It is very difficult indeed to carry out such a good pattern as the one he has made. When an artist has defects, weaknesses, or as they are called 'mannerisms', people imitate his mannerisms but do not imitate whatever good qualities he may have; these are always the last things to be imitated.

Many people confuse clever trickery of brush-work, or of pen-work, with real beauty of painting or drawing. The only way to learn to distinguish between the two is to do as I have advised you to: examine the works of really great artists. You will generally be surprised to find, on looking into their work, that it does not seem to be so clever after all—that the lines of a chalk drawing by Jean-François Millet are very ordinary, scribbly, untidy affairs really ; only the untidiness is just in the right place and of a kind which you do not notice unless you look for it.

     .   .   .   .

Perhaps some of you will become in your turn artists of value ; perhaps to you will be bequeathed the task of carrying art on, of fitting it to the future needs of society. Shall we wonder for a moment what will be, or better say what may be, the direction which art may take in future years ? To prophesy is dangerous work, and if in twenty or thirty years' time you re-read these pages, you must not be too hard on me if I am wrong. Well, let me say in a few words what it seems to me is going to happen. But first I must put in just a few lines about what has been happening recently and then go on, without interruption, to what I suppose will happen in the future. When I wrote *Relation in Art* about twelve years ago, I made a few prophecies ; they seem to have been fulfilled. This encourages me to go on with the profession of artistic fortune-teller !

     .   .   .   .

Let us first of all remember that somewhere about 1860 a little group of men in Paris began the movement known later as Impressionism. Manet was the chief of the group ; Monet, Sisley, Pissarro, Renoir, and others completed it. These men professed to paint effects of light and colour straight from Nature without troubling about all the recognized rules about picture-making, and they proposed to do away with the 'studio', 'academical' painting with the nice brown shadows, which was painted in a 'proper' way. To begin with they had a pretty hard time of it. Happily for them Monsieur Durand-Ruel bought their pictures in spite of the laughter of people in general, who always laugh at what they are too ignorant to understand. But as time went on these men revolutionized the painting of the whole Europeanized world, and Monsieur Durand-Ruel reaped the benefit of his early confidence by making a large fortune. The Impressionists looked at things and then put their brush-marks on the canvas just according to the 'impression' which they received from Nature, and without paying any attention to studio recipes about scumbling, and transparent tints for shadows, and painting over, and heaps of other things. They just sat down in front of the landscape and tried their best to give an impression of the light and the air and the colour of the scene in front of them without paying any attention to what people told them that a picture ought to be. Thirty, forty years passed, and the same kind of person who, in 1865, would have stupidly burst out laughing in front of a picture by Monet, began to pay very high prices for it. That is why I tell you not to listen to popular opinion about a living painter. Such popular opinion has nearly always been wrong. Such popular opinion admires artists who do what has already been done forty or fifty years ago. But such painters are not artists at all; an artist is an originator, a man who does what hasn't been done before. He who does what has been done before is only an imitator, and though what he does may have been good when it was invented, and done properly by the first-class man who invented it, the imitators—who are third-rate men, otherwise they wouldn't imitate—do it badly (I have already told you that an imitator always imitates the worst part of the man whom he copies—another reason why I do not wish you to copy, but to go straight to Nature).

At the same time as that at which the Impressionists worked, Cézanne worked too. But he did not by any means have the same ideas. While the Impressionists only saw light and air and colour and movement in a landscape, Cézanne saw solid built-up form. He saw a chestnut trunk like Figure 23. He was hardly anxious at all about light and bright and varied colour, but he was fearfully anxious about solidity and pattern. That is why in this book on Drawing I have often spoken about him.

Later, in the 'eighties' came along another very extraordinary painter called Van Gogh. He finished up by going mad, and then killed himself. No one would buy his pictures (you can see two of them in the Tate Gallery to-day). He hadn't enough to eat, which hurried on, and perhaps was the chief cause of, his madness (as it was, too, in the case of the great French etcher Méryon). Van Gogh—who was a Dutchman—paid very little attention to constructional form. He drew in an extraordinary way all the same. His drawing was very 'wrong', but no one has ever drawn in a more excited way. His pen-lines or his brush-marks seem to be alive with excitement; they hurry about the paper or the canvas, and seem to squirm with annoyance at being unable to become really alive. But his colour was his principal innovation. He wanted his colour to be as alive as all the rest. He made it as brilliant as he could. He did not, however, bother so very much about its being quite natural, although he always painted directly from Nature just like the Impressionists. He had learnt a lot of things from the Japanese, and always had a lot of decorative ideas at the back of his head.

With Cézanne on one side and Van Gogh on the other, the one worrying about the geometrical shape of things, and the building of them up solidly, the other about decorative colour and excited free drawing, excited even at the cost of being badly done, we have the two sources of the art of the first twenty-five years of the twentieth century. In about 1900 Henri Matisse began to use colour in a still more fantastic way than did Van Gogh, and began to pay even less attention to 'correct' drawing. He became also more frankly decorative still and did not very often worry about painting from Nature at all. He made up rhythms of form and colour to please himself. Then in about 1910, if I remember rightly, people like Picasso and Gleizes began to practise 'Cubism' (it was Matisse who gave it that name). They took up Cézanne's cone-sphere-cylinder doctrine and exaggerated it. They pretended to paint, not things themselves, but the impression which they, the artists, received from the underlying construction of those things. And their painting became altogether like a mixture of propositions out of Euclid. This was going too far. So, at about the end of the war, they began to say that they had only been doing this in order to learn how to draw, and that now they were going to draw 'properly'.

Well, the result of all this is now being felt. If there are no really great draughtsmen, at least the general level of draughtsmanship is very much higher than it used to be while Impressionism was in fashion. Some people are beginning even to draw quite well and in an interesting way. And the ugly brown and grey tints, mostly dirty, that came from the influence of the Cubists are fast disappearing again. The very latest school is dealing in agreeable, frank tints and clear, decided drawing, with a great leaning towards sculptural quality.

.   .   .   .

Now I think that this movement is going to go on; I think that it is the movement in which you will take part if you become artists. All around you you see a lot of mechanical forms, those of motor-cars, those of steel railway-bridges, those of steamboats. Your eyes get used to these shapes which are almost geometrical; you find them natural, the right thing, beautiful. Nature herself contains something of everything. I think you will believe it to be the right thing to do to exaggerate ever so little the 'mechanical' side of Nature, to remind us, ever so little, that the trunk of a chestnut tree is mostly cylindrical. Yet you won't go as far as the Cubists did ten years ago. I think that the tendency of Cézanne and the Cubists will now join with that of Van Gogh and Matisse to produce an art which shall contain the qualities of both, and that both will meet once more on the eternal ground of Nature. In the years round 1907 or 1908 Matisse painted things very far from their natural appearances. Then some time during the war we find him coming slowly back to the study from Nature,

and producing some very delicate colour studies, generally at Nice or somewhere else on the coast of the
Mediterranean. For whatever may be his failings as a
draughtsman, Matisse is a great colourist. So in the end,
you see, we all come back to Nature.

I think that drawing will become better and better, but
not at all like the drawing of people like the *Pre-Raphaelites*
for example, nor at all like the thing you might trace from
a photograph. It will always, as all successful art must,
have a sense of life, but on the other hand it will clearly
show the mechanical and geometrical construction of things,
their solid and possible being. That is another reason why
I have talked such a lot about the geometrical construction
of things, because I think you will be called upon to show
that you understand it. But here let me warn you against
a great mistake that a lot of silly people make who think
that to make a drawing with straight lines or with stiffly
curved lines is to make a constructional drawing. The
only way to make a constructional drawing is to understand your construction. A drawing made up of angular
lines and curves with no real knowledge behind them only
takes in the ignorant part of the public. The best thing on
which to learn constructive drawing is on the nude human
body; to that study you must go on if you mean to take
up drawing properly.

The Cubists went wrong, because they forgot too much
about certain qualities of beauty without which we cannot
find ourselves completely satisfied. The first and only
reason for a drawing is beautiful emotion; we must never
lose sight of this among theories about planes and straight

lines, and lines of force, and balance, and all sorts of other things.

.   .   .   .

'Yet', you will say on looking back through the pages of this book, 'he talks about beauty all the time ; but when we come to it he makes drawings like Figure 23, which looks more like a problem in geometry than anything I should ever dream of calling beautiful.' Perhaps you have seen some buildings which you are quite ready to call beautiful. Do you think that they came there one doesn't know how ? Do you think that they were built without a lot of business discussion, without a lot of disordered stone-yards, without mortar-beds, without scaffolding put up anyhow and tied together with old bits of rope ? Do you think that the inside of a painter's studio is always fitted up just like the interior of a luxurious apartment ? Some magnificent curtain that he may be painting is generally a dirty, worn-out rag with holes in it that he has picked up at a rag and bone merchant's. The arts of drawing and of painting are, after all, crafts just like building ; they have their calculations, their stone-yards, and their scaffolding, all of which are carefully put out of sight when the job is done and the picture, finished off, is put into its tidy frame. The trouble is that people don't seem to understand this. Perhaps it comes from the fact that the 'stone-yard' of a drawing is less evident than is a real builder's stone-yard, so people think that it doesn't exist at all. People never take up amateur building, amateur mortar-mixing as a hobby. Who was the last amateur bricklayer whom you met ?   But because they think that it is a much easier and simpler affair to make lines on a piece of paper, every one cheerfully spends two shillings on a sketch-book. As a matter of fact brick-laying and house-building is play beside learning to draw properly; quite a few months' apprenticeship will enable you to build a house (of course I am not talking about pro-ducing a great masterpiece in architecture), but it will take many, many months' 'apprenticeship', combined with innate gift, before you will produce a drawing with worth in it.

This is the kind of vague idea about being more or less 'clever at drawing' which floods us with so many millions of weak, flimsy drawings (?). People don't realize that a drawing must, in the artist's mind, be as firmly established, built up, based on knowledge, as a house, and that you can no more build up a drawing without scaffolding than you can a house. If you don't do your work properly your wall won't stand up, nor will your drawing either. It is all very well to have an unlimited amount of senti-ment, to feel very convinced about the beauty of such and such a view, of such and such a play of light on a piece of Still Life. Such feeling, such sentiment you must have—I don't deny it. I finished *The Way to Sketch* with these words : 'A sketch is a statement of emotion. If you have no emotion to state, your sketch has no reason for existence.'

I am not here going to contradict what I said there ; but I am going to call your attention to the fact that all the difficulty comes in with the word 'statement'. How are you going to make this 'statement'? How are you going to build it up? This book contains a very few of the things which you must know about the *trade* of 'building up' drawing 'statements', with a view to their being beautiful *when they are done*. Unfortunately the mortar-mixing and the scaffolding are not quite so beautiful as we will hope the result is going to be. That is why, while talking about beauty, I was obliged to make a lot of diagrams which are often, to say the least of it, next door to ugly. But if you don't get these strong, ugly facts hidden away, like the steel girders of a modern building, within the very being of your beautiful drawing, it will never be beautiful; it can only be weak, perhaps pretty, always flimsy and valueless. Beauty and delicacy are never weak and flimsy. They are always strong, healthy, lithe, active. The delicacy which you put into your work must be placed over a strong and sufficient framework. When your framework is sturdy, put as much delicacy of rhythm and balance, as much gracious sweetness of curve as you are capable of imagining, on the top of it. Finish is nothing else but exquisite refinement of observation, writing down of new exquisite delicacies observed. Worthless draughtsmen replace this fine observing by a general tidying up.

But do not think that this study of constructional facts is the same thing as sitting down to make a 'shaded drawing of a sphere' in order to 'learn to draw' in a 'drawing class'. I don't want you to do that; I want you to start out with the idea of wishing to express the beauty of things around you. Then, with this idea firmly fixed in your mind, I want you to take the trouble to find out, as far as you can, why these things seem to be beautiful to you. I want you to understand that unless they fit in with certain geometrical and mechanical facts they will be neither true nor beautiful, and I want you to learn all you can about these facts and their application. This is a very different thing from sitting down stupidly to 'copy' one of those horrible white-painted cones or cylinders which one too often finds in a drawing class, and which I would like to see thrown on the rubbish-heap.

.   .   .   .

At the beginning of this book I quoted three suggestive lines from Robert Browning's poetry. I feel inclined here, almost at the end, to quote one or two others. Here they are; they are taken from ' Old Pictures in Florence ' :

> And fine as the beak of a young beccaccia
>   The Campanile, the Duomo's fit ally,
> Shall soar up in gold full fifty braccia,
>   Completing Florence, as Florence Italy.
>
> Shall I be alive that morning the scaffold
>   Is broken away, and the long-pent fire,
> Like the golden hope of the world, unbaffled
>   Springs from its sleep, and up goes the spire . . .?

So when the seeing things as cones and spheres, as perspective constructions, as anatomies of bone and muscle, as almost coldly calculated arrangements of light and shade, as almost mechanical balancings of objects, as buildings up of blocks,—when all this *necessary* scaffold is broken away, the long-pent fire of Beauty, like the golden hope of the world, unbaffled must spring from its sleep, and crown our work with its true, its only justification.

.   .   .   .

So now, as a parting word, I tell you to take up your pencil and any odd sheet of paper, and to go and scribble down anything which seems to suggest to you a beautiful pattern. Scribble from a table, from a pile of books, from the graceful branch of a tree, from the curiously shaped shadow on the wall, from a beam of westering light. But always try to find out all you can about what you are scribbling from ; how it is built up, how it is grown, how it is arranged, not only sideways but to and from you. Store up in your mind the knowledge that you collect in this way. It is this knowledge which will, from day to day, enable you to draw with more certainty, or, what is the same thing, to observe with more sureness and more rapidity. The more facts we observe, the more we begin to understand the great, simple laws which govern them ; and, understanding these laws, the easier it becomes for us to add new facts to our store of the appearances of Nature. The larger your store of knowledge concerning the construction of things and the appearances of that construction, the better draughtsman you will be. Drawing is nothing else. So don't ask me to set you exercises to 'do'. Go and 'do' what you like, so long as you are sure that it makes a good pattern. If, while you are at work, you find that you are mistaken, and that the pattern is not good, leave off at once, and if you think you see now (which you often will) how you ought to have thought of the pattern, take a new piece of paper and begin all over again. It is not the drawing that matters, it is learning to SEE.

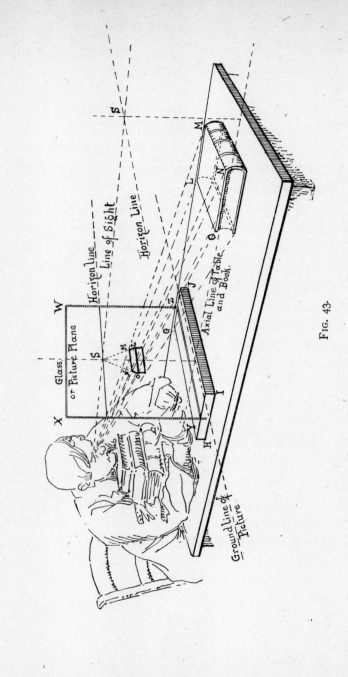

FIG. 43.

APPENDIX

CONCERNING PERSPECTIVE

Reprinted from *The Art and Craft of Drawing*.

A FREQUENT fault of writers on perspective is to present the matter in an unnecessarily arid and abstract way. A beginner will certainly get a better grip of the subject by following the experimental method of study at the start. Let him either look through the window, or better still set a pane of glass upright (Fig. 43) in a saw-cut YZ made in a board GHIJ, and place the apparatus on a table at some little distance from its edge. At the edge of the table let him pile up three or four books, and rest his chin on them, while he looks through the pane of glass at another book lying on the table a foot or eighteen inches beyond the glass, one edge of the book being parallel to the glass, and the book being placed centrally.[1] Figure 43 shows in LMNO approximately what he will see as the perspective shape of the book. The lines LM, MN, NO, OL, should be now traced on the glass with a brush holding some colour just too thick to run down the upright glass. The other lines should be drawn in, so as to complete the *perspective image* of the book on the *picture plane* of the glass. Either before tracing the image of the book, or now, the height of the eye above the

---

[1] In all these instructions I am carefully avoiding the use of exact geometric phraseology. The reader not used to mathematical texts would rather be confused than aided by such precision.

table should have been, or should be, exactly measured ; and great care should be taken, throughout the tracing, not to move the eye from its place. These operations being terminated the eye may be moved.

From the table upwards measure on the glass the height of the eye, and at that height draw with the brush the horizontal line HH'. This line is called the Horizon Line of the picture that we have drawn. Now continue the lines LM and ON upwards on the glass. If the work has been done carefully enough, these two lines prolonged will meet in the point S which will fall on the Horizon Line (Fig. 44). This point S is termed the *Point of Sight,* and is exactly 'opposite' the eye. The line HH' is called the Horizon Line because, if there be a sea horizon depicted in the drawing, it will lie exactly on this line, which is at the height of the eye, or, if it be preferred, on the same horizontal plane as the eye. That is why when we go up in a balloon or an aeroplane, the horizon always appears to be on our level, and consequently the earth seems to be hollowed out below our feet. This, also, is the fact expressed in Tennyson's 'hollows *crowned* by summer sea'; as an artist he treats of the appearance, and not of the reality of the scene ; for, of course, really the sea lay below the level of the edges of the hollows, hence could not 'crown' them, as it appears to do to an observer standing upright in a shallow depression of the dunes.

In the symmetrical arrangement just studied the point S—called the Point of Sight because a perpendicular from it to the surface of the glass runs through the observer's eye—unites in itself this property and also the one of

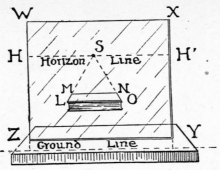

FIG. 44.

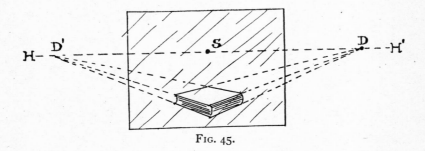

FIG. 45.

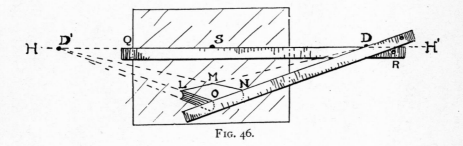

FIG. 46.

being the point to which the lines of the book sides converge. If, however, the book be not placed squarely and centrally in the system, the result is not quite the same. Let us now lay our book, still flat on the table, but with its edges making angles of 45° with the Picture Plane (that is, let us turn it through half a right angle). Repeat the tracing on the glass ; draw the Horizon Line as before, but this time measure, and note as well, the distance of the eye from the glass or Picture Plane. Figure 45 will represent our new result. When we now try to prolong the lines LM and ON, we find that, unless our eye has been placed remarkably close to the glass, our prolongations at once run off the glass without meeting. But if we lay a lath QR (Fig. 46) along the Horizon Line, and another straight edge along ON and LM, we discover that all three prolonged lines, HH', LM, and ON, meet now in a same point D on the prolongation of HH'. This point D is known as the Distance Point, because, as may be observed by measurement, it lies at exactly the same distance from the Point of Sight as does the point S from the eye. In other words, the length SD is the distance at which the observer is supposed to be placed when he looks at the picture. The choice of this length plays a very important part in picture making. It should then be remembered that the Distance Point lies on the Horizon Line, and is the point at which intersect all lines which lie in reality at 45° to the plane of the picture. If the lines OL and NM be prolonged in a similar way they will be found to intersect at D' at the same distance the other side of S.

The points S and D are two particular instances of what are called Vanishing Points, so termed because really parallel lines seem to disappear in some such point when they are drawn in perspective. S and D are special instances because they are respectively the Vanishing Points of lines perpendicular and 'half perpendicular' to the Picture Plane. Parallel lines making other real angles with the Picture Plane will have Vanishing Points of their own, which will, however, always lie on the Horizon Line so long as the original lines are horizontal, whether they are above or below the height of the eye.

GLOSSARY

ACROPOLIS. Rock dominating Athens, the capital of Greece. The Parthenon, the Erechtheion, and other temples were built on the Acropolis, which served as citadel to the town in ancient times.

AMMONITE. Fossil shell, related to the nautilus, belonging to the cephalopods (or 'head-foots'). All the species of ammonites are extinct, having only belonged to the Secondary period.

BAUX, LES. Town in the south of France. Almost entirely in ruins. Formerly very important. Department of Les Bouches-du-Rhône. Interesting Renaissance architecture.

BAUXITE. Aluminium ore. So called from Les Baux, where it is exploited. Hydrated oxide of aluminium, generally stained red with oxide of iron.

CALCAREOUS TERTIARY ROCK. A chalky form of sedimentary rock belonging to the latest but one geological period. The rock in question is soft and may be sawn. Limestone is of similar composition, but older and harder.

CAMPANILE. Italian word pronounced 'campaneelay'. It means a bell-tower. In Italy the bell-tower is often separated from the church. The campanile of Giotto at Florence is very celebrated. It is entirely covered with marble.

CÉZANNE. A French painter who is responsible for the greater part of the modern development of painting (see p. 139). He was born at Aix in Provence in 1839 and died there in 1906.

CHAVANNES, PUVIS DE. See Puvis de Chavannes.

CLAUDE LORRAIN. Real name Claude Gelée. Born 1600 in Lorraine. Studied Nature untiringly. Many of his drawings are now in the British Museum. Was a friend of Poussin. Turner imitated his 'Liber Studiorum' from the 'Liber Veritatis' of Claude. Died 1682.

CLAUDE MONET. Modern French painter of Impressionist school. Born 1840 in Paris. Died December 5, 1926.

CONTÉ. A French pencil-maker. But the word is usually understood to mean a very black chalk pencil, a speciality of the firm.

DAUMIER. A celebrated French caricaturist. Born at Marseilles in 1808. Died blind at Valmondois near Paris in 1879. His drawing was very powerful, sometimes recalling that of Michelangelo. He had a considerable influence on Jean-François Millet, whose 'Men sawing a Trunk' shows it very clearly. Daumier used very strong light and shade.

DETAIL. Term meaning all sorts of smaller and unimportant forms in a drawing, such as twigs, leaves, small stones, and so on.

DILIGENCE. French stage-coach. Pronounced something like 'dele-zhons'.

DISTANCE POINT. See p. 73 for explanation.

FRIEZE. The flat part of a building a little way above a row of columns and below the cornice. But it is often understood to mean a band of decoration along the upper part of a wall.

GLEIZES. A contemporary French painter. One of the foremost Cubists.

GODOSHI. The Japanese name of Wou Tao-tseu ; see lower down.

HORIZON LINE. For explanation see pp. 57 and 150.

HORIZONTALITY. When a thing is quite flat and level.

ICTINOS. The architect of the Parthenon. Lived in the 5th century B.C.

IMPRESSIONISTS. A school of French painters from Nature. See p. 137.

INGRES. A French painter. Born at Montluçon in 1780. Died in 1881 at Paris. Remarkable for the high finish and sculptural quality of his work, which may be studied in the Louvre. A slightly ribbed charcoal drawing-paper is named after him.

INTIMITY. Privacy. But used by painters for expressing a rendering of the sentiment of private life. The school of *Les Intimistes* painted such subjects as gatherings at table, or by the fireside, or based the sentiment of their paintings on such quiet feeling.

LEONARDO DA VINCI. Great Italian painter. Born in 1452 near Florence (Italy). Died in France in 1519. A very universal genius and great draughtsman. He was also interested in the science of his time. He has left a great number of manuscripts, treating of art, anatomy, and various speculations. He was one of the first to use strong light and shade.

LIANG K'AI. A Chinese painter. Lived in the first half of the 13th century. Sung epoch.

MANET. One of the original Impressionists. He usually painted figures rather than landscape. Remarkably certain and clear painting, suggestive of light and air. Died before the others in 1883. He was born in Paris in 1833.

MANNERISM. A certain artificial trick that an artist employs. Term generally used when the trick has become 'a way of doing things' which the artist applies in season and out of season, and which becomes somewhat annoying.

MATISSE, HENRI. Contemporary painter, and very fine colourist in an unexpected and decorative way. His drawing is less masterly.

MÉRYON. French etcher. Born 1821. Died 1868. May be studied in the Print Room, British Museum.

MICHELANGELO. Born in 1475 at Castel Caprese in Tuscany (Italy). Great sculptor and the painter of the frescoes of the vault of the Sistine Chapel at Rome. He died in Rome 1564 and was buried in Florence. His family name was Buonarroti.

MICHELET. A paper used for drawing in charcoal. It is slightly ribbed.

MILLET, JEAN-FRANÇOIS. French painter. Born in 1814, near Cherbourg. Died in 1875. The celebrated painter of the 'Angelus' and many other peasant subjects.

MONET. See Claude Monet.

MOU-HSI. Chinese painter. Lived about 1250 A.D. Very varied in his technique. A great master.

NEOLITHIC. The later age of stone, before the discovery of the metals. The date of the close of this age varies from country to country. We shall not be perhaps far wrong in placing it in Europe somewhere a little over 2,000 years B.C. It was preceded by the older stone age, or the Palaeolithic.

PARALLELS. Lines which are always at the same distance from one another, and which never meet however far you carry them on.

PARTHENON. The great temple on the Acropolis at Athens, erected by Ictinos and Pheidias (by order of Pericles) to Athene Parthenos. It is the most celebrated example of a 'Doric' temple.

PEDIMENT. The triangular shape above the columns on the front of a Greek temple.

PERSPECTIVE. The way of making things look solid although they are drawn on a flat piece of paper.

PHEIDIAS. Great Greek sculptor who lived at Athens in the 5th century before Christ. The sculpture of the Parthenon is, most of it, by him. It is nearly all in the British Museum to-day.

PICASSO. A modern Spanish painter. One of the originators of Cubism.

PIERO DELLA FRANCESCA. Tuscan painter (Italy) 1420 (1415 ?)-1492. One of the first to study perspective. Some very fine frescoes at Arezzo.

PIERO DI COSIMO. Born in Florence 1462. Died in 1521. May be studied in the National Gallery.

PLESIOSAURUS. An extinct reptile with a long neck. Its fossil remains are found in the Secondary Jurassic deposits.

PTERODACTYL. An extinct flying reptile. Its remains are also found in the Jurassic deposits.

PUVIS DE CHAVANNES. One of the last great French artists. Born in 1824. Died 1898. Was a great master of mural (wall) painting; which, however, he executed almost always in oil paint and not in fresco.

REFRACTION. The break in the direction taken by a beam of light when it leaves one transparent medium and enters another. The seeming bend in a stick which you put slantwise into water is due to refraction.

REMBRANDT. Great Dutch painter. Born at Leyden in 1605. Died in great poverty in 1669 in Amsterdam. His mastery of light and shade can be studied in the National Gallery.

RHYTHM, RHYTHMIC SEQUENCE. Effect produced in music or poetry by the ' following on ' of stresses in order. Sequence is ' following on '.

SCUMBLING. Rubbing on fairly dry opaque colour with a brush, to produce ' soft ' effects, and generally to soften off previous painting.

SECONDARY ROCKS. The rocks which compose the earth's surface have been divided by geologists into five periods of age : the oldest are the Volcanic and Pre-Cambrian ; then come the Primary ; the Secondary ; the Tertiary ; and finally the Quaternary, which bring us up to the recent formations of the present day.

SEDIMENTARY ROCKS. Rocks originally formed from mud at the bottom of the sea or a lake. They are distinguished from Igneous or Volcanic rocks, which have been melted.

SESSHŪ. Celebrated Japanese painter, who studied the Chinese masters a great deal (he went to China). He lived from 1420 to 1506. He was a most varied painter, and a great master of technique. One of his finest paintings was done with a feather brush.

STEREOSCOPE. An instrument which allows us to look, at the same time, at two photographs, taken from slightly different points of view which were the same distance apart as the eyes are. We get one impression from the two photographs, which impression seems to us to be one received from solid objects.

STILL LIFE. Inanimate objects (though flowers are included) arranged as the subject of a picture. Glass, porcelain, books, drapery, flowers (usually cut) are the most habitual still-life subjects.

STRATIFICATION. The layers that we see in some sedimentary rocks, and due to their being laid down from slightly differing mud deposits.

SYMMETRICAL. The same on each side.

TECHNIQUE. The way in which an art is carried out. The different methods of producing a work of art.

TITIAN. Great Venetian painter. May be studied in the National Gallery. Born at Cadore, near Venice, in 1477. Died, at the age of ninety-nine, in 1576; and painted right up to the last. He was a great colourist, but less great as a draughtsman.

TURNER. Great English landscape painter. May be studied in the Tate Gallery, London. Born in 1775. Died in 1851. Born and died in London. Invented modern brilliant colour.

VALUES. The relative lightness or darkness of a tint or colour. See p. 62.

VAN GOGH. A recent Dutch painter. Born in 1853 at Groot Zundert. Killed himself at Auvers-sur-Oise in France in 1890.

VANISHING POINT. See pp. 72, 75, and 153.

VELASQUEZ. Spanish painter. Born at Seville in 1599. Died at Madrid in 1660. Remarkably realistic painter. May be studied in the National Gallery.

VISUAL ANGLE. The angle formed by the rays of light which come from the opposite ends of an object and meet at the eye.

VOLCANIC ROCKS. Rocks which have been melted inside the earth. Also rocks made of ash thrown out by a volcano.

WASHING OUT. In water-colour, taking out a tint by washing with a brush and clean water. Part washing out obtains, on suitable paper, special effects.

WOLFF. Pencil-maker. Generally applied to the carbon pencils made by the firm. They give greyer and more delicate blacks and greys than do Conté pencils.

WOU TAO-TSEU. A great Chinese artist who lived in the 8th century after Christ. It is not quite certain whether we still possess any of his work, or whether we only possess copies of it. His work and that of other Chinese artists may be studied in the Print Room of the British Museum. A great number of Chinese and Japanese master-pieces are reproduced in the Japanese publication known as the *Kokka*. Much may be learnt from them.

INDEX

Acropolis : 84, 123–124, 155.
advice : 122.
aerial perspective : 60-64, 94.
aesthetics : x, xiii, 113.
air : 61.
ammonite : 34, 155.
angles : 85–86.
arrangement : 15, 19 ; see 'composition', 'pattern', 'spacing', &c.

background : 4.
balance : 18–21, 27–30, 41, 44, 85–87, 90, 105-107, 133.
beauty : vii, xiii, xv, 83–87, 103, 117, 124, 134, 142-146.
binocular or stereoscopic vision : 98–101.
branches : 82, 85, 105.
bread : 49.
British Museum : 30, 84.
Browning, Robert : xvi, 121, 146.
brush : 49, 52–53, 92.

Causses : 56.
Cavallerie, La : 56, 123, 127.
certainty : 52, 98.
Cézanne, Paul : 35, 54, 65, 83, 102–103, 114, 116, 135–136, 139–141, 155.
charcoal : 49.
cherry tree : 130–133.
China : xiii, 27, 35, 50, 92, 109, 134, 157, 160.
Chinese ink, 107, 123.
choice : 6-7, 12 passim, and see 'importance'.
circle in perspective : 71, 74-76, 81.
Claude Lorrain : 30-32, 35, 38-45, 52, 66-67, 82, 91, 112, 114, 131, 133, 155.
comparison : 94-95.
composition : 29-46, 92, 110.
construction : vii, 76, 77-92, 142.
contrast : 16.
copying : xiv, 23-24, 28, 35, 77.
Corsica : 78.
craft : 143.
cube in perspective : 74.
'cubic' shapes : 88.
Cubist : 27, 140-142, 156.
cylinder in perspective : 71-76, 79-83.

Daumier : 99, 156.
decoration : 27-28, 37, 133 ; see 'pattern'.
diagrams : 77.
distance : 65, 92, 94.
— point : 73, 152-153.
Douros : 43.
dragon : 109.
drawing and beauty : vii, xiv-xv, 84, 134, 143-146.
drudgery : vii, 7.
Durand-Ruel : 138.

effect : xii.
Egypt : xiii, 55.
emotion : xiii, 97, 103-104, 124, 142, 144.
enthusiasm : 103-104.
environment : x.

fatigue : 7, 24.
'figure' work : 70.
finish : xii. 11, 68, 91, 103, 120-121, 145.
flatness : 65-66, 77, 99, 106, 111 ; see 'solidity'.
force : 109.
foreground : 65, 93-95.
France, Anatole : xiv.
free-hand drawing : 22.
frontispiece : 14.
fun : 14.
future : 137-143.

geology : 34, 155, 157-160.
geometrical shapes : 82-90.
glass, pane of : 73, 149-153.
Gleizes : 140, 156.
Godoshi : 78, 156 ; see Wou Tao-tseu.
Greece : 27, 84, 123-124, 134, 155, 157-158.
ground-plan : 23, 25, 106.
growth : 83, 85.

head, drawing out of : 2, 9, 51.
Horace : xv.
Horizon Line : 55-59, 61, 64, 70-76, 79-80, 88, 150-153.

Ictinos : 84–85, 156.
illustrators : 99.
imagination : viii, ix.
imitation : 28, 139.
importance : 6, 11–13, 25, 30–31, 54, 116, 124 *passim*.
Impressionists : 1, 137–139, 156.
Indian ink : 49, 50, 52.
india-rubber : xv, 37, 47, 49, 53, 91, 118.
'Ingres' paper : 49, 156.
interest : 19–20, 24, 33–35.
interesting arrangement : 27–30, 94, 112.
intimity : 28, 156.
Italian primitives : 68, 155, 157.

Japan : 92, 109, 140, 159.
joining up : 40.
joy : 24.

key of colour : 21.
Kokka : 160.

leaving out : 19–20, 44, 105, 114.
Leonardo da Vinci : 23, 43, 62, 86, 91, 134, 156.
Les Baux : 107, 126, 155.
Liang K'ai : 121, 157.
life : 85, 89, 91.
light and shade : xii, 9, 123, 125–126.
lighting : 3, 64.
line : xii, 38, 42–44, 46, 91, 111, 113, 123.
look at the model : 5, 7.
luminosity : 15.

Manet, Édouard : 35, 137, 157.
mannerism : 136, 157.
mass : 32–33, 113.
materials : 47–53, 107.
Matisse, Henri : 140–142, 157.
mechanics : 86.
Méryon : 139, 157.
metope : 84.
Michelangelo : xv, 45, 78, 156–157.
'Michelet' paper : 49, 157.
'middle distance' : 39, 65, 92, 94.
Millet, Jean-François : 35, 137, 156–157.
minerals : 34.
modern art : vii, 135–143.
Monet, Claude : xi, 137, 155.
Mou-hsi : 35–37, 157.
movement : 114–115.
music : 28, 38, 83.

Nature : xii, xiii, 8, 13, 19, 23, 53, 58, 78, 85, 87, 96–97, 103–106, 112, 137–142, 147.
neolithic : 107, 157.

observation : ix, 5, 7–8, 13, 51.
originality : 138.
ornament : 24, 26, 43.
outline : 11, 123.

paper : 8, 47–48.
parallel lines : 55–59, 64, 157.
Parthenon : 84, 123, 157.
pattern : 3, 19–21, 30, 32, 35, 39, 40, 42, 44, 92–95, 105–107, 110–113, 117–133.
pediment : 84, 158.
pen : 48, 95, 115.
pencil : 49, 62, 92, 107, 115, 155.
perseverance : xii, 117–118.
perspective : 54–76, 149–153, 158.
Pheidias : 84–85, 158.
photograph : 18–20, 92, 97–99, 103–105, 128–133.
Picasso, Pablo : 140, 158.
picture plane : 72, 73, 149–150, 153.
Piero della Francesca : 125, 158.
Piero di Cosimo : 125, 158.
pine tree : 109–116.
Pissarro : 137.
planes : xii, 87, 90.
plaquemines : 36.
plesiosaurus : 34, 158.
plum tree : 109.
poetry : 28.
point of sight : 72–73, 75, 150–153.
portrait : 28.
'pot-boilers' : 68.
primitive art : vii–ix.
prism : 90.
pterodactyl : 34, 158.
Puvis de Chavannes : 78, 158.

Rabelais : xiv.
reason of sketch : 16, 144.
reflection : 9–10.
refraction : 4, 158.
Relation in Art : 137.
Rembrandt Van Ryn : 35, 78, 91, 125, 134, 136, 158.
Renoir : 137.

rhythm : 18–21, 38, 83, 90, 113, 158, *passim.*
rubbing out : xv, 7–9, 53.

scribbling : 1–4, 23, 30, 35, 38, 43, 45–46, 98, 112, 117, 124–126, 147.
scumbling : 138, 158.
seeing : vii, xii, 1–2, 7, 9–10, 62, 147.
— flat : 96.
— solidly : see 'solidity'.
Sesshū : 121, 159.
shadow : 3–6, 9–10, 14, 23, 64, 105, 147.
shapes of things : 54–76, 98.
sheet of paper : 34, 44.
simple subjects : 25–26, 36.
Sisley : 137.
sketch and photograph : 18–20.
solidity : xii, 23, 36, 54–76, 90, 98–103, 106.
South Kensington Museum : 99.
spacing : 36.
square in perspective : 74–76.
stability : xii, 91–92.
stereoscope : 98, 159.
Still Life : 3, 159
stratification of rocks : 34, 159.
subject : 24–46 *passim.*
suggestion : 6 7, 28.
suppleness : xii, 84, 85, 90.
surface : 36.
symmetry : 29.

technique : 52, 122–130, 159.
Tennyson : 150.
tension : 91.

thinking and doing : 6, 24, 37, 77, 115.
tidiness : xii, xv, 9, 22, 26, 43, 91–92, 115, 137.
tiger : 109.
Titian : 35, 159.
tools : 47.
tree trunk : 79, 114, 116.
trick : 136.
Turner : 23, 93, 120–121, 134, 159.
Tuscan School : 125.

unity : 40.

values : 62–65, 111, 159.
Van Gogh : 139–141, 159.
Vanishing Point : 55–57, 72–76, 81, 88.
Velasquez : 136, 159.
Via Appia : 57.
'views' : 93–94.
volume : xii, 110 ; see 'mass'.

wash-drawing : 50, 123.
water-colour : 50.
way to draw : 48.
Way to Sketch, The : 15, 144.
'weight' : 41.
what to draw : 22–46.
— — with : 47–53.
white, Chinese : 107.
'Why ?' : 16, 20.
Wolff pencil : 49, 160.
work : 26.
Wou Tao-tseu : 43, 78, 156, 160.

Zola : xiv.

Printed in England at the OXFORD UNIVERSITY PRESS
By John Johnson Printer to the University